Rebuttal to the Rogue

Malia Litman

Rebuttal to the Rogue

Cover Art by Ben Vincent
Dallas, Texas

Book Design by Falcon Books
San Ramon, California

ISBN: 978-0-615-33495-0

PRINTED IN THE UNITED STATES OF AMERICA

Dedication

Rebuttal to the Rogue is dedicated to the multitude of women who worked to elect Barack Obama as the 44th President of the United States. Some gave of their time, some gave money, and millions voted. Some were professional women, some were "soccer moms," and some were both. To each of you, whether your contribution was great or small, you should be proud. Sarah Palin was an embarrassment to us on the campaign trail, but she will not be an embarrassment to us in the White House.

Table of Contents

Prologue

January 8, 2008 was the New Hampshire primary. The significance of the New Hampshire primary is not its electoral votes, which are few. The importance of this primary lies in its position as the *first* primary. The victor in the New Hampshire primary gains the advantage of momentum and publicity. Hillary Clinton won in New Hampshire. Many perceived that this victory of Hillary was predictable, and a sign of things to come. Barack Obama could have been discouraged. Instead he gave one of the most powerful speeches of the entire campaign. In the face of loss, Barack Obama didn't lose hope. He seemed to know that if women had the opportunity to evaluate him, we, in our wisdom, would elect him. He inspired us with these three simple words: *"Yes We Can!"* Barack Obama told the people of America:

> "...There is something happening. There's something happening when Americans who are young in age and in spirit, who've never participated in politics before, turn out in numbers we have never seen because they know in their hearts that this time must be different.

> ...But always remember that, no matter what obstacles stand in our way, nothing can stand in the way of the power of millions of voices calling for change....

> ...Yes, we can. Yes, we can. Yes, we can.

It was a creed written into the founding documents that declared the destiny of a nation: Yes, we can....

...It was the call... of women who reached for the ballot...Yes, we can, to justice and equality."[1]

This speech has become known as the "*Yes, We Can*" speech. A video was made of this speech by will.i.am, and posted on You-Tube on Feb 2, 2008.[2] That video has been watched over twenty-two million times on various internet sites.[3]

Having listened to these powerful words on that January night, I immediately became committed to making a difference. Yet, I am just now beginning to appreciate the full impact of the message. Never before had I participated in politics. To my surprise, others felt as passionately about the candidate as I. The women I met during the campaign were inspirational. People turned out in record numbers to support Barack Obama; to campaign for him, to raise money, and to vote for our first African American President.

The first meeting I attended was held at a football stadium, to accommodate the hundreds of volunteers. People turned out in droves, even though it was only the primary, and even though the meeting was being held *deep in the heart of Texas*. At every step, there were women all around, taking an active role in the election of Barack Obama. As I embarked upon this journey, I met men and women, gay and straight people, young and old, Black, White, Asian, and Hispanic, and people of every hair color, eye color, weight, and height imaginable. My focus was not the women, but the number of people who were volunteering, who were fired up and ready to go. The only objective was the election of Barack Obama. It was our common purpose that brought us together. It is our President, Barack Obama who gave us hope, and who now inspires us.

Not until working at the early voting location, in the general election, surrounded by women, did I begin to focus on the variety and sheer number of women with whom I had worked during the campaign. We shared a common belief; change was essential to the future of our country. Our motivations were the same, and different. Each of us had been inspired by Barack Obama to believe that change could happen. It was of little consequence to us that a woman was a candidate in the primary. It was important only because she was our adversary. At the time we began, we had no way of knowing that John McCain would choose a woman as a running mate. If we had known in the beginning that Sarah Palin might have been our next President, our level of commitment would have been even greater. We didn't perceive that we were fighting for "women's rights," or that we were part of a movement to liberate women. It was despair over the state of our country that motivated us to work. It was Barack Obama who inspired us to "reach for the ballot" and to motivate others to do the same. It was a man who gave us hope. It was a man who made us believe that we could make a difference. We are appreciative of Barack Obama, and the men who inspired us. We gratefully acknowledge those men in our lives who respect us. Women "reached for the ballot" in record numbers, and constituted the majority of voters in the election of 2008! Today women constitute the majority of the electorate in the U.S. Given the life expectancy of men and women in our country, that "majority" will only grow larger.

Much publicity has surrounded this election. Yet little has been said about the impact of women in this election. Sarah Palin has quit her job as Governor, but still seems to attract media attention. It's time the 35,900,000 women who voted for Barack Obama speak out. We didn't elect John McCain and Sarah Palin, with good reason. Women made the difference in this election. Women turned out in record numbers to vote, in this election, and we, in our wisdom, elected the candidate who was most closely aligned with our interests. The candidate we chose just happened to be the male candidate, who selected a male Vice-President. One day we will elect our first female President, and/or Vice-President, but we must be patient. We must wait until the best candidate happens to be a woman. When she appears I will be there to support her. I will wait for the "right" female candidate. Until then I will celebrate the liberation of women. I will applaud the wisdom of women. We have found our voices, and proved by our action that women are the most powerful political force in the United States of America.

Sarah Palin was NOT our candidate, and she will NOT be our candidate in any future election. We expect and demand more! She is not an example of a competent professional woman and she is not an example of a mother dedicated to doing her best for her kids. John McCain exercised very poor judgment, or no judgment at all, when he selected Sarah Palin. By selecting Sarah Palin, Senator McCain demonstrated that winning an election was more important to him than the security of our country. Given his age and medical history, John should have put a significant amount of time, effort, and energy into the selection of a Vice-President. Even if Sarah Palin was unable to appreciate how ill-equipped she was to serve as Vice-President, John McCain knew better. To put Sarah Palin in a position that she could have been the President of the United States of America was criminal. Shame on you John McCain!

It has been almost an entire century since women won the right to vote.[4] I have lived only half of that time. I have witnessed discrimination of women in multiple arenas. It is because of that discrimination, and personal challenges in my life that I am particularly sensitive to any woman who would interfere with our struggle to gain respect. Sarah Palin was an embarrassment to women around the country…young, old, Black, white, Jewish, Christian, Republicans, Democrats, professionals, and "stay-at-home moms." However John McCain's attitude toward women, as illustrated by the nomination of Sarah Palin, is what troubles me most. Even if John McCain wanted to select a woman for political reasons, Sarah was certainly not the most qualified woman he could find to be his running mate. The fact that there were five female Republican Senators and three female Republican Governors at the time of Sarah's nomination is a clear indication that McCain's priority was not competency, education, or experience. Did John think that appearance was the critical attribute for a female public official? Obviously John McCain's standards for judging a woman are different than the majority of voters in 2008. People around the country objected to Sarah Palin, not because she is a woman, but because of her competency, or lack thereof. I object to any person who runs for the highest office in the land, and risks the safety and security of our country by nominating a person like Sarah Palin for the position of Vice-President.

Rebuttal to the Rogue is my personal attempt to ensure that no one confuses competent professional women, or dedicated mothers with Sarah Palin. The sign on the public restroom door may be the same for both Sarah and me, but that is our only commonality. The similarities between Sarah Palin and competent professional women, or dedicated mothers, begin and end, at the chromosomal level. Women in America include doctors, nurses, principals, teachers, attorneys, legal assistants, butchers, cashiers, Senators, housekeepers, professionals and women who stay at home to raise the next generation of Feminists. Sarah Palin doesn't represent the majority of us. We demonstrated by our votes for Barack Obama that John McCain was foolish to think that women in America would associate Sarah Palin with Hillary Clinton. For greater than 100 years women have fought to be respected as at least equal to our male counter-parts. The election of 2008 demonstrated that the fight is not over, but women are winning. By our votes we have proved that the majority of American women stand by our conviction that gender should never be the determinative factor in any election. Women proved by our votes for Obama, and against McCain/Palin, that we are not hypocrites. Sarah Palin characterizes herself as a Rogue. We agree…she is a scoundrel.

Chapter 1

The "Rogue"

For over one year Sarah Palin has been the subject of media attention, news broadcasts, internet sites, feature articles in magazines, and her biographies have appeared on the shelves of our favorite book stores. She has been a constant source of material for comedy routines on Saturday Night Live, David Letterman,[5] Jay Leno, Jimmy Fallon, Conan O'Brien, and Bill Maher. We could always count on funny and amazing news stories about Sarah Palin from Chris Matthews, Keith Olberman, and Rachel Maddow. During the campaign these jokes and commentaries were both frightening and embarrassing. It was hard to laugh as long as there was any possibility that this person, who seemed to be so clueless, could become our next President. Until Sarah Palin became the Vice-Presidential nominee of John McCain, it seemed impossible that any candidate for President or Vice-President could possibly convey such a lack of understanding and intelligence. In the span of two-and-a-half months Sarah Palin established a new low for clueless politicians. We can only hope that politicians will learn from this experience, and refrain from choosing a running mate on the basis of attractiveness.

Some women were offended by the treatment of Sarah in the press. Yet it seems to be the job of the press to challenge anyone who might run for political office. Maybe the problem was that there was simply so much to work with in the case of Sarah Palin. Some women identified with her because she advertised herself as a "hockey mom." Some women liked her because she was attractive, adorned herself with pretty clothes on the campaign trail, wore lipstick, had five children, and because she was a contender in the Miss Alaska beauty pageant. However some of us were offended that she was touted as the "woman's choice" or that she somehow represented the "American woman." I have been a Registered nurse, a senior partner at a large Dallas law-firm, and a stay-at-home mom. She doesn't represent either the professional women or the stay-at-home-moms who have crossed my path. The interviews of Sarah on the campaign trail were only funny if we could be sure she would never be our leader. Now that the election is over, I had hoped Sarah would simply disappear, and we would be left with the funny jokes. She is no longer the Governor of Alaska and she is no longer the running-mate of John McCain. Yet, we don't seem to be able to avoid her. Surely there are more pressing news stories than the opinion of the ex-Governor of Alaska, about herself. Surely our time could be better spent doing anything other than watching or reading about what Sarah Palin thinks,... about Sarah Palin. Women must speak out loudly and emphatically to ensure that all of America recognizes that the majority of women in America do not identify with Sarah Palin. We must set the record straight, so that there can be no confusion or misconception, about the candidate for whom the majority of women in America voted in 2008.

Barack Obama will be my candidate in the election of 2012. Perhaps the easiest way to ensure his success in 2012 would be to have Sarah Palin as his adversary. However as much as I would like to see Barack Obama re-elected, it should not be at the expense of the image of the American woman. Women in this country are smarter, more politically savvy, more educated, better mothers, and worthy of more respect than Sarah Palin. Sarah is pretty and well proportioned, but not competent to lead. Her education is minimal; her experience is limited, and her judgment is sorely deficient. Sarah Palin is a living example of everything women have worked so hard to overcome. On the campaign trail, she was usually allowed to give only pre-approved speeches, written by someone else,…probably a man. She was not allowed, or able, to "think" for herself. Her interviews with Katie Couric and Charles Gibson would have been funny if they had been scripts on Saturday Night Live, instead of actual interviews with a person who could have potentially been the President. In fact, actual quotes of Sarah were used in comedy routines, simply because they were so ridiculous. How could John McCain do this to America? How could the Republican Party sanction her nomination when there were so many more qualified female Republicans? Did the Republican Party overlook the 5 female Republican Senators,[6] and the three other Republican female Governors?[7] If the goal was to nominate a female, was the Republican Party suggesting that Sarah Palin was the best they could find? Was Sarah the most intelligent, experienced, educated, and competent female available? If Governor Palin was the "best" they could find, the selection of Sarah speaks volumes about the Republican Party's attitude about women. If Sarah Palin was the most worthy female candidate the Republican Party could find, we can only conclude that the leaders of the party were looking for the most attractive female, not the most competent or the most intelligent. For me, I am much more concerned with the intelligence, demeanor, leadership qualities, integrity, and personal values of any candidate, male or female, that might earn my vote. Before considering any candidate's positions on social issues, they must first establish that they are competent to lead. When John McCain nominated Sarah Palin to be his Vice-Presidential running mate, I blinked. I can't stop blinking.

It has been more than one year since the election of 2008, and I am still being subjected to Sarah Palin. I am fed up! I won't tolerate being bombarded by the hypocrisy of Sarah Palin, without responding. John McCain, and the Republican Party insulted all the women of America through the selection of a woman who is attractive, but lacks the qualifications and intellect to be a world leader. If the Republican Party respected women, its leaders would have ensured that the first woman selected as a Vice-Presidential candidate was the most professionally competent person they could find; not necessarily the prettiest. I am not a celebrity or news reporter. I know only what I have read and have not performed any independent investigation of Sarah Palin. If a stay-at-home mom is capable of reading and learning about Sarah Palin, surely John McCain could have done the same. Oh wait a minute, I forgot…he doesn't use a computer. Maybe one of the young guys on his staff could have helped him. **IF** he had any young women on his staff, I know they could have found what I have found on their computers.

Many may disagree with the statements contained herein. However because Grandmother Palin has been given many opportunities to share her views with the American public, the contrary view should also be shared. This is my **Rebuttal to the Rogue**. You be the judge.

Sarah chose as the title for her new book, *Going Rogue: An American Life*. Until I heard about this book, words that came to mind to describe Sarah Palin had not included "Rogue." My home edition of Webster's dictionary defines a "rogue" as 1. " a wandering beggar or tramp; vagabond," and 2. "a rascal; scoundrel"[8] Maybe Sarah is in fact a "rascal or scoundrel?" But only a clueless Rogue or scoundrel would describe herself in the title of a book on the nation's best seller list by a term which means a scoundrel suggesting that she is a "mean, immoral, or wicked person."[9]

In my mind an equally accurate description would be "Hypocrite." My dictionary defines a "hypocrite" as "a person who pretends to be what he or she is not; one who pretends to be better than is really so, or to be pious, virtuous, etc. without really being so."[10] While many politicians are hypocrites, never before has a politician been so obvious about saying one thing, and doing another. Sarah Palin even assured the American public that "…the nice thing about running with John McCain is I can assure you he doesn't tell one thing to one group and then turns around and tells something else to another group, …"[11] This comment was predictive of Palin's comments when she said one thing and then did another. Because so many of her statements left us in shock and outright disbelief, we were forced to take issue with EVERYTHING Sarah Palin said.

How could Sarah say to the American public that she is not a "QUITTER" in the very same interview in which she was discussing her resignation as the Governor of Alaska? This "non-quitter" (1) quit her job on the City Council of Wasilla,[12] (2) quit her job on the Oil and Gas Conservation Commission, [13] and (3) quit her job as Governor of Alaska.[14] Maybe Sarah doesn't have a dictionary? Maybe Sarah has never used a dictionary? My dictionary defines "quitting" to mean to abandon, cease, discontinue, or to leave.[15] Governor Palin abandoned her job as Governor, ceased going to work, discontinued any responsibility for the wellbeing of the citizens of Alaska, and left her office as Governor. She is a quitter. How foolish does she think we are? Does she really believe that we will believe her when she says one thing while she does the opposite? If Sarah Palin had become the Vice- President of our country, do you think she would have gotten tired, quit, and decided to go fishing, and still tried to convince us that she is not a "quitter?"[16] It is humiliating to the citizens of this country for a candidate to tell us one thing and do the opposite in the very same speech. How gullible does she think we are? Maybe she doesn't get it, but I do! It is even more objectionable when the hypocrite is our first Republican female candidate for President or Vice-President. Does Sarah think we are that ignorant, or is she simply foolish enough to fail to realize the hypocrisy in her actions?

Chapter 2

Who is Sarah Palin?

As I sat in front of the television in August of 2008, the Republican Convention was of great interest to me. Never before had I taken an active role in political campaigns, but this time was different. No longer could I complain about the multitude of problems facing our country if I was unwilling to become an active participant. I had worked for the Barack Obama campaign since January of 2008, so I was particularly interested in the Republican convention and John McCain's choice for Vice-President. Many people were potential candidates to serve as the Vice-Presidential running-mate of John McCain. A woman named "Sarah Palin" was not one on my radar. Who was Sarah Palin? What qualified her to be the potential Vice-President of this great country? The answer became clear. She was not qualified! As time has passed, the answer has become even more obvious. The notion that Sarah Palin was an example of the all-American woman is humiliating. As a professional and as a mother she is unimpressive. Most of the mothers and professional women I know would be more qualified, more educated, and more competent leaders than Sarah. She is an embarrassment to women. She lacks the intelligence and leadership qualities of most professional women. She lacks the dedication and commitment of most stay-at-home mothers. She won the Miss Wasilla beauty pageant, but most don't consider a beauty queen award from a small town in Alaska to be a credential we value in our elected officials. She advertised herself as a "hockey mom." Few kids play hockey in Dallas Texas. Most play soccer. The "soccer moms" I know would have a better understanding of their own limitations than Governor Palin seems to have.

The Republican Convention was my introduction to Sarah Palin. I wish we had never been introduced. While the choice of Sarah Palin probably ensured the election of Barack Obama, I am still disappointed that the image of women in America has been tarnished by the nomination of a woman so clearly incompetent. John McCain did a huge disservice to the women of America to nominate a woman based upon her appearance, and little else. Republicans and Democrats are often unable to agree on anything, but many in both parties agreed that the selection of Sarah Palin as John McCain's running mate was a fatal mistake.

Thanksgiving

At Thanksgiving every year my house is the locale for our family feast of turkey and dressing. The ages of the family members around our table in the fall of 2008 were as diverse as our political views. My niece was 2; mom was 74. Some might characterize my political views as "liberal." Phil, my brother, a Database Administrator who lives in L.A., shares my view of civil rights and politics. We each have a wicked, irreverent, sense of humor and similar views about political adversaries. Frank, my older brother, attended Georgia Tech on a ROTC scholarship, is a retired Air Force pilot, and now is a Senior Check-pilot with a commercial airline. Cindy is eleven years younger than me. She graduated with a bachelor's degree from the school of Broadcast Journalism, at Oklahoma State University. Cindy worked as the producer of the news at one of the top three news stations in

Tulsa until she had children. At that point in her professional life, she like her older sister, was confronted with what she found to be an impossible balancing act of trying to be a successful mother while pursing her career. Even when Cindy's baby had an ear infection, people in Tulsa still turned on the T.V., expecting to see the news. Cindy's youngest child is now 6 years old. Cindy has changed her career path to accommodate her kids. She is a professional photographer, but only works when her children are in school, or late at night after the kids have gone to sleep. Frank and Cindy are companions on the political spectrum, being staunch conservatives. Steve is a medical doctor living in Norman Oklahoma. Steve would be considered a political moderate. While he still resides in Oklahoma, he lives in a college town, so his political views are a little more moderate than the typical Sooner. On Thanksgiving in 2008, the political views of my family fairly represented those of the entire country. In an effort to avoid the heart-burn that would inevitably result from a family political discussion during Thanksgiving dinner, we agreed that politics was "off-limits." However, by the time we got to the pumpkin pie, we broke our own rule. Nothing was "off-limits."

A few things were not controversial. We agreed that the country faced incredible challenges on November 4, 2008. Race and gender were not the motivating reasons for any of our votes. Three of us had voted for Obama, and only two had voted for McCain. All five of us were stunned by McCain's choice of Sarah Palin as his running mate! Phil and I were much more outspoken than Cindy and Frank, but we all perceived Sarah Palin to be an inappropriate choice for Vice-President. It was obvious to all that McCain thought that the selection of Palin would result in attracting the "women's vote." We agreed that it was foolish to think that women in our country, who had voted for

Hillary in the Primary, would become Palin supporters. In spite of our best efforts, the only similarity we could identify between Hillary Rodham Clinton and Sarah Palin was anatomical. Because Hillary had not showcased her anatomical features in a Beauty Pageant,[17] the degree of any similarity would be speculative.

When we talked about the Katie Couric interviews of Palin, Frank snickered, slowly shaking his head, and covered his eyes. As much as he wanted to see a Republican in the White House, even he was embarrassed by Sarah Palin. What was it about Sarah Palin that my brothers, sister, and I found so objectionable, given our diverse political views? We found that we could agree on a couple of things: (1) Sarah Palin is a living example of the "Peter Principle" (i.e. people rise to their highest level of incompetence) and (2) Sarah Palin's T.V. interview, with a turkey in the background being slaughtered, was hilarious. [18]

My siblings and I were focused on Sarah's lack of education, intellect, experience, political savvy, knowledge of world affairs, and knowledge of world geography. However Cindy and I were both amazed that Sarah had been selected to attract the "women's vote." Cindy voted for McCain, *in spite of* Sarah Palin. I worked harder to ensure the election of Barack Obama *because of* Sarah Palin. Cindy and I felt we were forced to evaluate Sarah Palin's success as a mother, or lack thereof, given the fact that she chose to characterize herself as a "hockey mom," and given the fact that she used her Down-Syndrome child as a prop, or trophy at the Republican Convention.[19] Cindy and I had each given up our established careers to devote ourselves to raising our children. We each have 3 kids, not five. We each began exploring part-time options after the birth of our first child. Neither of us was successful in our attempt to balance part-time careers and full-time families. Neither of us was serving as Governor, had 5 children, had a "special-needs child," had an unmarried pregnant teenage daughter, and neither of us held an elected political position such as Governor of Alaska. Both of us found it disingenuous that Todd was making it all work because he was a "stay-at-home dad." We learned that:

1. Todd worked full time for British Petroleum on the North Slope, requiring him to be gone for an entire week, every other week.[20]

2. Todd worked every summer as a fisherman, working in Bristol Bay.[21]

3. Todd spent "a good part of every winter preparing for the Iron Dog.[22]

4. That was Todd standing behind Sarah at most of the rallies. If he was a "stay-at-home dad" why would he need between $20,000 and $40,000 worth of suits?[23] Do you know any father who changes dirty diapers …in his suits?

5. If Todd was the "stay at home" dad, why wasn't he at home with the kids?

As diverse as our political views might be, Cindy and I found it difficult to believe that the Palin kids were getting the love and attention that they needed…and deserved. If Todd was truly a stay-at-home dad, we would respect the family's choice. Yet the presence of Todd on the campaign trail made it obvious that he was not devoting himself to the kids. As mothers, we both recognize that none of us has mastered the art of being the perfect parent. Some parents have to work to ensure food and shelter for their kids. However, if that was the motivation of Sarah Palin, Cindy and I hadn't heard that story. We know that the birth of a child is only the beginning. Giving birth to a Down-Syndrome child is no more difficult than giving birth to a "normal" child. The difference is the challenge of caring for that child, day after day, probably for the rest of your life, knowing that the child will always have limitations. We can admire Sarah and Todd for their willingness to undertake this challenge, but we then expect that at least one of them should provide for Trig the time, attention, love and support he needs. Having been raised Catholic, both Cindy and I respect Sarah's right to choose to give birth to a Down-Syndrome child, but we then expect her to honor her obligation to care for Trig. We both found it offensive for Sarah to choose to have a "special needs child" and then demand that another child of hers provide the care needed by the "special needs child."[24] The night of the Republican Convention is not my idea of an "appropriate environment" for ANY 4 month-old child. It was past his bedtime![25] Even one of Sarah's close, long time friends, Curtis, the person for whom the hockey center was named, felt that Sarah's career might be getting in the way of raising her children.[26] Sarah Palin is tenacious and we should never underestimate her resolve to accomplish a goal.[27] However we should not confuse tenacity, or prolificacy, with competency. Sarah Palin falls short of our expectations as a competent leader and as a competent mother.

The ABC's of Sarah Palin

In evaluating a person as the potential Vice-President of the United States, we necessarily hold the candidate to the same standard as a candidate for President. Because of John McCain's age, and medical history,[28] his choice of a Vice-Presidential running mate was critical. Intelligence and education are at the top of my list for the person who would earn my vote. These characteristics are of primary importance, and must be evaluated even before I consider the candidate's positions on social or political issues.

Sarah Palin's education was noticeably deficient. In high school her grades were "good but not that high."[29] While Sarah attended college, her record was not one of a student who sought academic prowess. Many students, including my own children, spend hundreds of hours learning about potential colleges, gathering information about the professors, visiting colleges, interviewing college counselors, meeting with college representatives, and attempting to find the best college available to them to suit their academic and professional goals. Not Sarah. The primary motivating factor for Sarah in choosing a college was the identification of the college where she and her 3 friends could all gain admission, and enjoy the weather.[30] The University of Hawaii admitted all 4 girls, and would have great weather…or so the girls thought.[31] Whether it was because they forgot to do their homework, or the unexpected rain they encountered in Hawaii, or both, the girls withdrew during their first semester.[32] The girls were able to take advantage of the liberal laws in Hawaii regarding marijuana, so at least the experience wasn't a total loss.[33] Even if Sarah did not find time to learn to surf the three waves of Feminism while in Hawaii, at least she found some form of recreation.

After attending 5 colleges in the next five years, Sarah finally obtained a Bachelor's Degree in Broadcast Journalism at the University of Idaho in Moscow.[34] Maybe Sarah's lack of focus on the importance of education was of little concern to John McCain, since it was clearly not his strong suit.[35] It does concern me. The apparent lack of emphasis on education seems to be a value shared by the entire Palin family. Todd, Sarah's husband, doesn't have a college degree.[36] Track, her oldest child, didn't earn a college degree.[37] Bristol is 18, has a child, and while she was able to graduate from high school,[38] she is giving up on her pre-baby education plans for a college degree in nursing.[39] Levi, the father of Sarah's grandson, has dropped out of high school.[40]

Years of experience and accomplishment in political office might help to fill the void if a candidate had less than a stellar academic record. However neither Sarah's academic record, nor her record as an elected official, could be described as "stellar." "Adequate" would be overly kind. A more appropriate description of her record as an elected official might be, "…live…from Alaska, it's the Peter Principle."

Live from Wasilla…

Sarah Palin served two three-year terms as the Mayor of Wasilla, Alaska, and a small town of about 6300 residents.[41] She held this position from 1996-2002. One of the first things she did as mayor of the small town was to talk with the town librarian about the possibility of banning books.[42] Given her lack of interest in education, and her limited understanding of Constitutional Law, perhaps this isn't too surprising. Was it her religious affiliation that caused her to believe that it was part of *her* job to monitor the books *other* people read? What is surprising is that Sarah felt that she was the best person to monitor what other people read, since it's questionable what she reads…..or, does she read at all?!? Remember the Katie Couric interview?[43]

The book that gave rise to the controversy was *Daddy's Roommate* which is the story of a young boy whose divorced father moved in with his gay partner.[44] Maybe it was Sarah's view regarding homosexuality that caused her to object to this book.[45] Whatever her motivation, it is clear that it was not because she personally read the book and objected to its content. She refused to review the book herself.[46] She must have acted on "faith." When it was clear that she would not be successful in banning the book, she made sure the book was transferred to a fringe community where "hardly any people live."[47]

Interestingly, *Daddy's Roommate* is a picture book targeting young children who may not understand the dynamics of a man who divorces his wife to live with his gay roommate.[48] Certainly this picture book, with a total of 13 sentences, is not intended to be of assistance to an adult trying to resolve homosexual tendencies. The obvious intent is to help educate a *child* trying to understand the dynamics of a homosexual relationship in his family.[49] If Mayor Palin was successful in preventing anyone from reading this book, it was a child who suffered. **IF** Sarah had read the book she would have known that the mother in the book explained that "Being gay is just one more kind of love. And love is the best kind of happiness."[50]

Sarah Palin is a formidable adversary. If she can't accomplish her goal directly, she may accomplish it another way, with or without violating the U.S. Constitution. When she recognized that it would not be possible to proceed directly in banning the book, and in manipulating the librarian to act as Mayor Palin directed, Sarah accomplished her goal another way. Sarah was able to stop construction of the new library.[51] Sarah fired the librarian. Even though the librarian was reinstated, the librarian ultimately resigned.[52] Certainly we would never fault the librarian for recognizing how difficult it would be to continue working for her boss. Even if you disagree with the opinions expressed herein, surely you would agree that the First Amendment, which guarantees your right, and mine, of free speech, is controlling. You and I each have the right to express our opinions; at least we are supposed to have that right. Any politician who accomplishes an unconstitutional goal, directly or indirectly, is abusing her power.

Politicians may lie, steal, and cheat. The headlines of the last 20 years are replete with political scandal. Yet the worst crime against the electorate is abuse of power. Abuse of power is the wrongful use of power to facilitate a personal objective.[53] When we elect a person to office we give a sacred gift of our trust. When a politician wrongfully uses the power that we have bestowed upon her, that politician violates our trust. We empower that person with control and influence so that she may lead. When the politician abuses her power she hurts every voter. It is especially painful when the abuse of power is the subversion of the very Constitution she is sworn to protect. The Alaskans who elected Sarah Palin as their mayor were left injured when she left office. Palin violated their trust. While she was not able to actually ban books, she accomplished the goal by using her power to limit funding for the construction of the new library, by causing the librarian to resign, and ensuring that the book in question was sent to a remote location where the people of Wasilla would not have easy access to it. Sarah did indirectly what she was prohibited from doing directly. The book you are currently reading would have likely made the top of the list of "Sarah's Books to Ban." If she should ever be elected President of the U.S., I will surely go to jail, or be a fugitive. Sarah Palin made it clear that in her view, the hockey center was more important to the people of Wasilla than a new library. Why would they need to read books when there was hockey to play?

The Hockey Center: A Costly Mistake

During the time Sarah served as mayor, the single largest project undertaken by the city was the construction of a new hockey center.[54] As a "hockey mom," a nice place to go to watch hockey would be a predictable priority. Even without a law degree, the average person would not commit millions of dollars to the construction of a building on property where there was any question as to the ownership of, or title to, the land. Sarah Palin did.[55] The property where she wanted to build the new hockey center was owned by someone else. Sarah **KNEW** a citizen owned the land and refused to sell the land, which was appraised at $125,000.00.[56] Given the proposed timetable and site selection for the hockey center, if the city were to proceed as Sarah advocated, they would have to begin construction of the hockey center on property the city did not own. The city followed Sarah's lead. They trusted her and "made a leap of faith."[57] They would later find that their "faith" in Sarah was misplaced. Because the city did not own the property before beginning construction, the small town of Wasilla had to pay the property owner and his attorney over $1,800,000.00.[58] This "leap of faith" cost Wasilla roughly $1,675,000.00, over and above the appraised cost of the land.

In her short time as Mayor of Wasilla, Sarah Palin wrongfully (1) attempted to force a citizen to give up his property, (2) wrongfully wasted tax-payer money to attempt to accomplish her personal goal, (3) inquired into the possibility of banning books that she considered to be inappropriate, even though she never read them, (4) caused the resignation of the librarian, and (5) limited the funding for the library. Is this the track record of the person anybody would want to become the President of the United States? I hope the people who supported her just didn't know. The Peter Principle suggests that people rise to their level of incompetence.[59] Sarah Palin as Mayor of Wasilla is a perfect example of the "Peter Principle."

Sarah Palin Doesn't Favor Earmarks…Except for Alaska

On the campaign trail last year, Governor Palin "sold herself as a crusading reformer who despised earmarks."[60] At the Republican convention she touted her record "as a reformer who worked to end the abuses of earmark spending in Congress."[61]

John McCain called the practice of doling out favors, often with scant oversight "disgraceful."[62] The hypocrisy of Sarah's Palin's comments regarding earmarks is obvious. In 2008, the year of the Republican Convention when she made her famous re-marks regarding earmarks, and being a maverick, Sarah Palin sent to Sen. Ted Stevens, a Republican in Alaska, a proposal for 31 earmarks totaling $197 million dollars, more per person than any other state.[63] Sarah's knowledge may be seriously limited in many areas, but earmarks is something she knows a lot about.

While Mayor of the small town of Wasilla, Sarah Palin hired a lobbyist in Washington D.C. [64] From the limited funds generated by the Wasilla tax dollars, Sarah paid the lobbyist $38,000.00 for the purpose of enlisting his help to obtain federal earmarks for Wasilla. [65] This time Wasilla hit the jack-pot! This "jack-pot" in-cluded various improvements for the small town of 6300 resi-dents at a cost to the U.S. taxpayers of $27,000,000.00.[66] As Governor, Sarah again advocated earmarks for Alaska. In Au-gust of 2006, Sarah advocated the building of a bridge that has become known as the "Bridge to Nowhere."[67] This name might be considered appropriate as the bridge was designed to con-nect the mainland of Alaska to an island with a total of 50 inhab-itants. [68] The cost to the United States tax-payers was estimated to be $233,000,000.00. [69] (this translates into a benefit to the in-habitants of this remote island of greater than $4,000,000.00 per resident). Sometime between August of 2006 and August of 2008 it became obvious that (1) the Bridge to Nowhere would not be built, and (2) Sarah's image as a "Maverick" would be better served to say "no-thanks" to the money for the bridge since it wasn't going to be built anyway, and it would be a catchy phrase to use in her acceptance speech at the Republican Convention.[70] Even though Sarah and John McCain indicated that they were not in favor of "earmarks" during the campaign, the state of

Alaska asked for $3.2 million dollars to study the genetics of harbor seals, and also requested money to study the mating habits of crabs.[71]

There has been a lot of controversy surrounding the comment made by Gov. Palin that she said "thanks, but no thanks" to the "Bridge to Nowhere."[72] Perhaps her perception of the need for the bridge really did change. Let's give her the benefit-of-the-doubt regarding the Bridge. Consider Sarah's involvement with the "Road to Nowhere." It's one thing to say that you don't advocate earmarks, and then request them. However the worst abuse is to request earmarks, have Congress approve the money, and then waste the money.

The story that most people heard was that Sarah Palin changed her position with regard to the Bridge to Nowhere, to suit her agenda at a later time. However the real incompetence, or corruption, relates to the building of the "Road to Nowhere."[73] When Congress originally approved the building of the "Bridge to Nowhere," Congress approved approximately $25,000,000 to build a road leading from the airport to the Bridge.[74] When the funding for the Bridge was withdrawn, Congress evidently overlooked the funds that had been allocated for the construction of the road leading to the Bridge. As Governor of Alaska, it was Sarah Palin who oversaw the use of federal funds to build the Road to Nowhere, and indicated that "yes" she was in support of the road.[75] According to the Alaska Transportation Priorities Project, a group promoting "sensible transportation systems in the state," the "Road to Nowhere" is an irresponsible waste.[76] The project received more than $100 million dollars in federal and state funding. This includes a $15,000,000.00 federal earmark and approximately 24 million dollars passed through to the state.[77] It didn't seem to matter that the road led to the edge of a cliff (where the Bridge had originally been planned to be built). At the time Sarah approved construction of the road it was expected to be totally useless.[78] Congress had already approved the money.[79] Why wouldn't Sarah proceed with the building of the road, whether anyone needed it or not?[80] The only possible motivation to suspend the project, halting the construction of the road, would be that Governor Palin wouldn't want to waste millions of dollars of U.S. taxpayer money. Since that didn't happen, she must have intended to waste our money! We can debate the merits of the Bridge to Nowhere, but there is no debate about this road. Once the construction of the Bridge was tabled, there was not even a purported reason for the road.[81] Could this be a trend emerging?

The road is still there and in great shape. It will likely still be in great shape when Bristol's baby is grown, because it won't suffer from the deterioration of a road that is used. Maybe this is the path we should suggest for Sarah Palin's political career?!

Let's rename the road...

The road leading to Nowhere!

(Proposed new name—
"Sarah's Road, Going Nowhere")[82]

Using a Public Office to Advance a Personal Agenda.

On another occasion, Sarah was wrong to use her position as an elected official to accomplish a personal goal, as determined by an Alaska legislative panel. The legislative panel investigating allegations of wrongdoing on the part of Sarah Palin in the "Trooper-Gate" matter found:

> "Gov. Palin knowingly permitted a situation to continue where impermissible pressure was placed on several subordinates in order to advance a personal agenda."[83]

The investigator's report states that Palin broke state ethics laws when she attempted to get State Trooper Mike Wooten, (her ex-brother in law) fired.[84] This was the finding, by Alaskan legislators, that their own Governor, Sarah Palin, used her political position in an unethical way, to accomplish a personal goal. If Sarah Palin, as a mayor and later as Governor, has a history of abusing power, and wasting tax payer money, why would we promote her? Why wouldn't we be very scared to allow her to stay in the office she currently occupied, much less promote her to the Oval Office? This isn't the type of "maverick" I want running our country. Maybe we should create Commandments for her so that she clearly understands what is expected of an elected official:

1. Thou shall not waste taxpayer money.

2. Thou shall not abuse power.

3. Thou shall not abridge a citizen's 1st Amendment Right to freedom of speech.

4. Thou shall not wrongfully take another's property.

I thought these commandments were understood, but maybe I should send her a copy of this book!

The Highest Level of Incompetence—McCain's V.P.

As the Mayor of Wasilla, we saw that Sarah Palin was not skilled at running the town, both from a fiscal standpoint, and as the protector of the constitutional rights of the citizens of Wasilla. As the Governor of Alaska, Sarah Palin demonstrated fiscal irresponsibility when she approved the building of the Road to Nowhere, and took advantage of her position and power to advance a personal agenda. The Peter Principle proved applicable a third time when John McCain chose Sarah Palin to be his Vice-Presidential running mate. For over 100 years women have been fighting for equal rights, fair pay, freedom from abuse, and for respect. Isn't it obvious that all women would look to our first female Vice-President or President as our leader, our role model, and hold her to the highest standard of public scrutiny, because she would be our representative? Wouldn't we care about the example she would set for women in our country? Why did John McCain's daughter, a conservative and a Republican, have difficulty endorsing Sarah Palin as the best candidate in 2012?[85] In the case of Sarah Palin, why were there so many unanswered questions? Certainly her political views were consistent with the mainstream thought in the Republican party. Weren't they?

Sarah must have known that by accepting the nomination as John McCain's running-mate that she, her immediate family, and all connected to her would necessarily be thrown into the spotlight. She had to know that, for better or worse, she and her family would become the focus of attention in the news every night until the election. Didn't she know that if people in her family were arrested, the public would be interested?[86] Wasn't she concerned that someone might find out that she had charged tax payers for the travel expenses of her children? Did she think we wouldn't care?[87]Did she think that it wouldn't matter if the person she trusted to lead her in prayer, her pastor, had been hunting "witches" in Africa?[88]I am confused! I have many unanswered questions:

- Why would Sarah Palin advertise herself as a "hockey mom" if she missed most of the games?[89]

- Why would "hockey moms" in Alaska who knew Sarah, make a video and post it on you-tube indicating their disapproval of Sarah Palin as a "hockey mom"?[90]

- Wasn't Todd, Sarah's husband, a member of the "Alaskan Independence party?" Wasn't Keith Vogel the leader of that party? Wasn't the Alaskan Independence Party the party that advocated succession of Alaska? Didn't Mr. Vogel say: "The fires of hell are frozen glaciers compared to my hatred for the American government, and I won't be buried under their damn flag." And didn't he also say: "I'm an Alaskan, not an American. I've got no use for America or her damn institutions."[91]

- Did Sarah even know what the Bush Doctrine was when she was interviewed by Charlie Gibson?[92]

- Why can't Sarah pronounce the word "nuclear"? Does she think it is spelled "nucular"?[93] If she can't even pronounce the word, should we trust her with the codes?

- Has she "bitten the hand of every person who extended theirs to her?"[94] Are those people afraid to say anything publically about her, because they fear retribution?[95]

- Why doesn't Sarah learn from her own mistakes? If she was pregnant when she "eloped," did she expect her daughter to internalize the value of "abstinence" better than she had herself?[96]

- If Sarah had political aspirations, and 4 children, why would she choose to get pregnant for a fifth time…at 44 years old?

- Sarah agreed to have an amniocentesis in the 13th week of her 5th pregnancy.[97] Isn't there a risk of spontaneous abortion with an amniocentesis? If you were opposed to abortion, regardless of the circumstances, why would you ever assume the risk of having an amniocentesis? Sarah has admitted that she considered an abortion following the information that her child would be a "special needs" child.[98] Regardless of her ultimate decision, the crucial consideration is that she contemplated her CHOICE. Implicit in the consideration of her CHOICE is the notion that some mothers might not make the same CHOICE. Some might not be ready to "embrace a child with special needs,"[99] especially if the mother had political aspirations, and four other children. The importance of the constitutional right identified by the U.S. Supreme Court in <u>Roe v. Wade</u> was that the pregnant woman, in the first trimester of pregnancy, should have a CHOICE. I wonder if it would have been harder for Sarah to make up her mind if she had been pregnant with the offspring of a rapist, or with her brother? I wonder if the reason she kept the pregnancy a secret for so long was that she wanted to keep her options open?

- Do you think Sarah would try to ban a book entitled *"Bristol's Baby"* from the libraries of Alaska? She is a proponent of abstinence before marriage, so we might expect that such a book would not be welcome.

- Why would any pregnant woman get on an airplane in Texas, bound for Alaska, AFTER her water had broken, knowing the flight would last at least 9 hours, and knowing it was her 5th child, and knowing that with each pregnancy the length of labor tends to be shorter?[100] I know when my mom went to the hospital for the labor and delivery of Cindy, her 5th child, time was not a luxury she had. The doctor who delivered Cindy was someone walking down the hall that mom didn't know, still in his sport coat, that the nurses grabbed and pulled into the room as Cindy was being born. Why wouldn't Sarah at least tell the airline, before boarding the plane, that she was in labor? Wouldn't that be important information for the airline to know before determining if it would be wise for her to become a passenger on that flight? What health risks would her Down Syndrome baby face if delivered on an airplane? Do you think Sarah was considering the impact on the other passengers on the plane of having a woman in labor on their plane? Do you think they have a "birthing chair" on planes?[101]

- If you were in labor with your fifth child, and had completed a 9 hour flight without yet giving birth, why would you get in a car and drive 51 minutes (according to MapQuest) to the hospital in Palmer Alaska, instead of going directly to the hospital in Anchorage?[102]

- Why would you agree to serve as the Vice-Presidential Candidate when your 17 year old daughter was 5 months pregnant?[103]

- Why does Governor Palin still advocate teaching only abstinence when her 17 year old unwed daughter has a child and her own daughter does not think teaching abstinence is "REALISTIC"?[104] If it didn't work for Sarah, and it didn't work for her daughter, does Sarah really think it will work for other teenage girls in Alaska? Does she feel it just doesn't matter whether her position is realistic? If she read newspapers she would find that teen pregnancy rates in the United States are the highest they have been since 1991.[105] One third of the teenage girls in the United States got pregnant before age 20 and more than 435,000 babies were born to women ages 15-19 in 2006.[106] At least one in four teenage girls in the United

States has a Sexually Transmitted Disease, which is more than 3 million teenage girls.[107] Don't women, especially Feminists, have an obligation to girls and young women to try to help prevent dependence upon parents or men? When a woman becomes dependent, that woman looses fundamental rights for herself, and potentially for her children. Maybe what Sarah advocates in public forums is different than what she does in private? She did allow her daughter Bristol (the one who was pregnant at the Republican convention) to live with her boyfriend, Levi Johnston (the father of Bristol's baby), in Sarah's home.[108] Is it possible that a politician might say one thing publically and do another in private?

- Was the contractor for the Wasilla Hockey Center the same one Sarah used on her new house? Did that contractor build the Hockey Center and Sarah's home at the same time? Why was Sarah in such a hurry to start construction of the hockey center, when she knew she didn't have title to the land?[109]

- Speaking of title to land…did Sarah get a title policy on her home when she bought the house that was located too close to the lake, and too close to the neighbor's property?[110] If Sarah didn't need a variance when she bought the house, why did the people trying to buy the house from her need a variance? The carport that was supposed to be taken down…the one that was still there in 2008….is it still there?

- Why did the Palin family give interviews after the election if they really wanted family matters to stay private?

- Why did the Palin family sell pictures of Bristol's baby? Do you think they should have asked more than $300,000 for the pictures?[111]

- Why have female relatives of the Palins been arrested?[112]

- Was Sarah Palin the most competent woman John McCain could find to nominate as the Vice-President, or just the prettiest? Do you think he was looking for a savvy, politically astute, educated, informed woman, to be his running mate...or did he just want a Beauty Queen? Having chosen a beauty queen, did John McCain expect her to speak, or to just look pretty? Do you think John McCain was mad at the Republican Party because they wouldn't approve his first two choices since those two people were PRO-CHOICE?[113] I wonder if they now regret that CHOICE?

- Why wouldn't McCain endorse Palin as a potential candidate for the Presidency in 2012?[114]

- Why won't John McCain's daughter Meghan endorse Sarah Palin as the Republican candidate for President of the United States in 2012?[115]

- Why were McCain's aides angry with Sarah after the election? Why would they characterize the shopping spree of Palin and her family as the "Wasilla hillbillies looting Neiman Marcus from coast to coast?"[116]

- Why were millions of American men and women offended by the selection of Sarah Palin as the potential Vice-President of the United States?

- If John McCain had been elected, died in office, and Sarah Palin had become President, who do you think she would have picked as her Vice President? Do you think she would pick a college graduate? Could she have picked Todd?[117]

- If Sarah doesn't read books, how is she going to write one?[118]

- If she needs help writing a book, why would Sarah Palin choose Lynn Vincent, someone associated with white supremacists, to write her book?[119]

- Do people in Sarah's church still speak in tongues?[120] Do you think they could translate this?

"I saw a upporters fo erryK. Od ouy hinkt I ma oingg ot ellh?"[121]

- Have you ever heard the saying *"Res Ipsa Loquiter?"* It's a Latin saying that I learned in law school. It means:

"The thing speaks for itself."

Sarah, John McCain's Nightmare

John McCain chose Sarah Palin as his running mate, surprising most Americans, at the Republican Convention, on August 28, 2008.[122] There was an initial bump in his popularity, and some women reacted favorably, simply because of the thrill of having a female Vice-President. However the "bump" was short-lived.[123] Time magazine reported on Oct 2, 2008 that the McCain campaign was being "hobbled" by Sarah Palin's Vice-Presidential candidacy.[124] In just a few days Palin sealed the deal for Barack Obama. Time magazine featured a picture of a protester's sign depicting Palin as a "Woman of Mass Destruction."[125] This title was earned in the Katie Couric interviews conducted in September and early October of 2008, when Palin's lack of education, understanding, experience, and insight were broadcast on national news.[126] Some of Palin's comments in that interview made the Yale Book of Quotations for 2008, which included:

1. "I can see Russia from my house!" Sarah Palin on her foreign-policy credentials as satirized by Tina Fey, NBC "Saturday Night Live" broadcast, Sept. 13, 2008.

2. "All of them, any of them that have been in front of me over all these years." Sarah Palin responding to Katie Couric asking her to specifically name newspapers or magazines she reads, CBS News interview Oct.1, 2008.[127]

It is interesting to note that McCain allowed Katie Couric, a pretty woman, to interview Palin. Was he thinking that a "pretty" woman wouldn't be smart enough to ask insightful questions? Did John think Katie would ask questions about make-up secrets, hair style tips, and wardrobe challenges? Again, the McCain campaign severely underestimated the intelligence of women, …interviewers and voters. "Gratitude" is the predominate emotion that I feel for the McCain campaign. It was their attitude and belief in the stupidity of women that sealed the deal! Who is the fool now?

Sarah is Not a Quitter?!?

On July 3, 2009 Sarah Palin declared her independence from "politics as usual"[128] by announcing that she would resign her elected position as Governor of Alaska, effective in late July.[129] I agree that by resigning her job as Governor, she was no longer a politician in the "usual" sense. While her resignation speech was "often-disjointed,"[130] her personal lawyer, Thomas Van Flein, explained that Sarah needed a break after being "on duty now for two and a half years solid."[131] After announcing her resignation Sarah went fishing.[132] While Sarah described herself as a fighter and "not a quitter,"[133] it's hard to understand how resigning the position of Governor could be viewed by an objective observer as "fighting" instead of quitting! Questions that logically follow include:

- Did Sarah resign as governor because she didn't want to admit that her popularity among the people of Alaska was on a steep decline?

Sarah's Approval Ratings in Alaska[134]

Date	Approval %
May 30, 2007	89%
June 21, 2007	93%
Nov. 4, 2007	83%
April 10, 2008	73%
May 17, 2008	69%
Aug. 29, 2008	64%
Oct. 7, 2008	63%
March 24, 2009	59.8%
May 5, 2009	54%

July 3, 2009 Sarah Palin announces that she will resign as Governor.[135]

- Did Sarah get her feelings hurt by the Vanity Fair article that reported… "many skilled veterans of the Republican Party—long regarded as the more adroit team in Presidential politics—keep loyally working for her election even after they privately realized **she was casual about the truth and totally unfit for the Vice-Presidency**?"[136]

- Was her resignation inspired by the fact that she could make far more money in the private sector than the estimated $125,000 she was making as the Governor?[137] Levi Johnston, the father of her grandson, who reportedly lived in Sarah's home, said Sarah… "talked about how nice it would be to take some of this money people had been offering us and you know just run with it, say 'forget everything else'"[138] Some reported she wanted as much as $11,000,000.00 for her memoirs.[139] She has already been paid a $1,250,000.00 "advance" by Harper Collins for her memoir, which is to have an initial print run of 1.5 million copies.[140] It seems that it is very profitable to be a Rogue, or a scoundrel.

- Was being the governor of Alaska too frustrating for Sarah?[141]

- Didn't Sarah resign from the City Council of Wasilla in 1995-96?[142]

- Didn't Sarah resign from the Oil and Gas Conservation Commission in 2004?[143]

- Is there a trend emerging? Is this the behavior of a person who fights, ...or quits?

- If elected President, Sarah would be our first female President. Would Sarah resign that job too,...and then go fishing? When the going gets tough, do the tough go fishing? If 2½ years was too long in the position of Governor, I wonder how long she would make it as President. Isn't the Presidential term 4 years? If the memoir of the Governor of Alaska is worth millions of dollars, after less than a full term, I wonder how much the memoir of a Vice-President or President might be worth after less than a full term?

- Is it possible she became exhausted from trying to keep her eyes open? I know she didn't blink when asked to run as Vice-President, but maybe she thought she shouldn't blink during the campaign too?[144]

- Did Sarah get worn out serving as Governor of Alaska, because of the challenging problems facing her as governor? I know she found it necessary to issue many proclamations during her short term as Governor of Alaska. The dangerous weeds in Alaska were just one such stress for the Governor:

'WHEREAS, Alaska is in a unique position to avoid the enormous cost of widespread invasive plants, now impacting all 48 contiguous states and Hawaii…"

NOW THEREFORE, I Sarah Palin, Governor of the state of Alaska, do hereby proclaim June 21-27 as the **Alaska Invasive Weeds Awareness Week**.[145]

- Were celebrities and comedians too much for Sarah? I found them all to be entertaining, but I could understand why Sarah might not have been laughing.

- Was Sarah surprised that columnists like Roger Simon reported:… "She is a dumb hick, a nobody from nowhere. She hunts moose with a chainsaw from the back of a snowmobile, or something. Just listen to her resignation speech….What a doofus!"?[146] If these reporters, celebrities, and comedians were mean-spirited, to the point of causing Sarah to resign as Governor, leaders of foreign countries might take note…saying something mean spirited to her.

Wasn't her experience as Governor of Alaska the only job that even arguably prepared Sarah for higher office? If she was Governor less than two years before being named by John McCain as his running mate, and her resignation was announced within months of the end of that campaign, did she really serve as Governor more than two years? Is a degree in Broadcast Journalism and service as Governor of Alaska for roughly two years, the kind of education and credentials we expect for the potential President of the United States?

Given the information available regarding Sarah Palin, it is easy to wonder about the reasons for Sarah's political ambition. A few things are clear. Sarah came from very modest beginnings.[147] Sarah and Todd were very limited financially from the time they were first married.[148] Even if Todd worked very hard, it was unlikely that Todd would ever achieve the financial success for which Sarah aspired, without Sarah's help. By seeking the office of Governor, her salary would exceed anything she could have made as the mayor of Wasilla. By seeking the position of Vice-President, she achieved national attention that could easily result in a financial windfall, as evidenced by the book offers, the price paid for grandchild photos, speaking engagements etc. Thus, if her goal was financial success, Sarah Palin has shown wisdom by resigning her office as Governor, and securing her financial future.[149] However ability to generate personal financial success is not the critical factor in determining the candidate for whom I will vote.

I have the Audacity to Hope that the citizens of America have gained wisdom from the election of 2008.[150] Women especially need to take necessary action to ensure that we never come so close to a national disaster as we did in November 2008. Perhaps we need to enact some requirements for a minimum level of education for all candidates for the President of the United States? Maybe there should be some type of standardized test. People have to take a test to get a driver's license in Texas, so why don't we require a test to determine if a person is fit to hold the highest office in the United States of America? The Presidential test might include geography, ethics, foreign relations, history, economics, political science, government, strategic defense, and women's studies. We should require any candidate to have a minimum IQ, be able to problem solve, and understand fundamental logic. Whatever requirements or test we might create in the future, I feel confident Sarah Palin would have to go back to school to pass such a test. Every voter in this country must first determine that a candidate is fit to lead, before we consider her positions on particular social issues. We must first view the candidates through the goggles we wear when surfing the waves of

Feminism. If the candidate doesn't come into focus through those goggles, we need not view any longer.

I don't blame Sarah for never learning to surf. I am sure it's too cold where Sarah lives for surfing. What disappoints me is that after almost a century of struggle to gain respect, the nomination of Sarah Palin was a set back for women. Sarah Palin is a woman who isn't "on our team." Instead of elevating the status of women in the country, she is an embarrassment. Instead of helping women break through the glass ceiling, she is adding another layer of glass. Her social values are not mine, but I respect her right to have values different from mine. The problem is that she seems to believe that all who hold values different than hers are not entitled to the same protections provided by the very Constitution she was sworn to uphold as Governor, and would have been required to protect as the Vice-President. Maybe Sarah should have taken a Constitutional Law class? Maybe Sarah would have benefitted from coming down with the flu when she was supposed to participate in the Miss Wasilla beauty contest?

Sarah would have been 11 years old in 1975, the year I was graduating from High School. I was playing the trumpet with all the boys in High School. When Sarah was in High School, she played the flute, which was typically thought to be a "girl's" instrument. The flute doesn't have a spit valve, and is a much daintier instrument than the trumpet. You can't wear lipstick while playing the trumpet and the spit valve on a trumpet has to be emptied regularly. Somehow I don't think the judges at the Miss America pageant envisioned the queen of femininity as a woman blowing on the cold metal mouthpiece of her trumpet, with a long string of viscous saliva hanging suspended in mid-air, from the spit valve. As a trumpet player, I learned to compete with the boys. The trumpet players were typically the musicians who played the melody, instead of the accompaniment. Maybe Sarah would have benefitted by having to take the lead? Maybe Sarah would have benefitted from the installment of a spit valve in her flute?

Chapter 3

Sarah's Folly—She Said What?

A person who is a hypocrite is usually clever enough to say one thing and do another…at a later time. Sarah Palin has been known to contradict herself in the very next sentence. Sometimes it takes a few days before we fully understand the hypocrisy in what she says. Maybe Sarah Palin isn't evil, but just clueless. Consider these actual quotes of Sarah Palin, her comments recorded on national television, and the reports of Levi Johnson, the father of Sarah's grandchild,[151] who lived with the Palin family for a time.

1. Feminism

Question: Do you consider yourself a Feminist?[152]

Palin's answer: I do. I'm a feminist who believes in equal rights. Someone who would not stand for oppression against women.[153]…I know that in a McCain–Palin administration we will not stand for any measure that would result in a woman being paid less than a man for equal work.…

Question: Why shouldn't the Ledbetter act (an act that "sort of lengthens the time a woman can sue her company if she's not getting equal pay for equal work") be in place?[154]

Palin's Answer: It would have turned into a boon for trial lawyers.[155]

2. Talking to Reporters

Question: Do you think the coverage of you has been sexist?
Palin's Answer: No, I don't....

Question: If that's the case, why haven't you been more accessible to reporters?

Palin's Answer: I am so happy to talk to reporters. My life is an open book, happy to do it and very happy for more opportunities to do so.[156]

3. The Government Bailout

Question: (by Katie Couric, when asked about the $700 billion government bailout of bad debt) Do you support it?

Palin's Answer: " I'm all about the position that America is in and that we have to look at a $700 billion bailout. And as Sen. McCain has said unless this nearly trillion dollar bailout is what it may end up to be, unless there are amendments in Paulson's proposal, really I don't believe that Americans are going to support this and we will not support this. The interesting thing in the last couple of days that I have seen is that Americans are waiting to see what John McCain will do on this proposal. They're not waiting to see what Barack Obama is going to do. Is he going to do this and see what way the political wind's blowing? They're waiting to see if John McCain will be able to see these amendments implemented in Paulson's proposal."[157]

Jack Cafferty of CNN commented on this incoherent answer:

"...I'm 65 years old and I have been covering politics for a long time...and that's one of the most pathetic pieces of tape I have ever seen from someone aspiring to one of the highest offices in this country."[158]

Jack explained that "there's a reason that the McCain campaign keeps Palin from the press." "If (her nomination) doesn't scare the hell out of you…it should."[159]

4. Reforming Wall Street

Question: You've said quote, "John McCain will reform the way Wall Street does business." Other than supporting stricter regulations of Fannie Mae and Freddie Mac two years ago, can you give us any more example of his leading the charge for more oversight?

Palin's Answer: "I think that the example that you just cited, with his warnings two years ago about Fannie and Freddie-that that's paramount. That's more than a heck of a lot of other senators and representatives did for us."

Question: But he's been in Congress for 26 years. He's been chairman of the powerful Commerce Committee. And he has almost always sided with less regulation, not more….I'm going to ask you one more time – not to belabor the point. Specific examples in his 26 years of pushing for more regulation.

Palin's Answer: "I'll try to find you some and I'll bring them to you."[160]

5. Reading done by Sarah

Question: In preparing for this conversation, a lot of our viewers …and Internet users wanted to know why you did not get a passport until the last year. And they wondered if that indicated a lack of interest and curiosity in the world.

Palin's Answer: "…The way that I have understood the world is through education, through books, through mediums that have provided me a lot of perspective on the world."[161]

Question: And when it comes to establishing your worldview, I was curious, what newspapers and magazines did you regularly read before you were tapped for this to stay informed and to understand the world?

Palin's Answer: "I've read most of them, again with a great appreciation for the press, for the media."

Question: What, specifically?

Palin's Answer: "Um, all of them, any of them that have been in front of me all these years."

Question: Can you name a few?

Palin's Answer: "I have a vast variety of sources where we get our news, too. Alaska isn't a foreign country, where it's kind of suggested, "Wow, how could you keep in touch with what the rest of Washington, D.C., may be thinking when you live up there in Alaska? Believe me, Alaska is like a microcosm of America."[162]

Levi Johnston indicated that Sarah doesn't read much at all.[163] Even though newspapers were delivered to her address, Levi never saw her reading them.[164]

6. Foreign Policy Experience

Question: You've cited Alaska's proximity to Russia as part of your foreign policy experience. What did you mean by that?

Palin's Answer: "That Alaska has a very narrow maritime border between a foreign country, Russia, and, on our other side, the land-boundary that we have with Canada. It's funny that a comment like that was kinda made to....I don't know, you know....reporters...."

Question: Well, explain to me why that enhances your foreign-policy credentials.

Answer: "Well, it certainly does, because our, our next-door neighbors are foreign countries, there in the state that I am the executive of. ...As Putin rears his head and comes into the air space of the United States of America, where do they go? It's Alaska. It's just right over the border. It is from Alaska that we send those out to make sure that an eye is being kept on this very powerful nation, Russia, because they are right there, they are right next to our state."[165]

7. Freedom of the Press

Palin Speech: "...And first, some straight talk for some, just some in the media because another right protected for all of us is freedom of the press...So how 'bout in honor of the American soldier, ya quit makin' things up...and one other thing for the media, our new governor has a very nice family too, so leave his kids alone."[166]

(See discussion herein of Sarah's attitudes regarding freedom of Press (sic...speech) when it pertains to books for kids regarding homosexuality. See also, later discussion regarding money made by the Palin family when they did NOT keep children private, and sold pictures of Sarah's grandchildren for hundreds of thousands of dollars.)

8. The Outcome of the 2008 Election

Dobson asks if she is discouraged at all, even hearing the polls showing McCain-Palin is behind:

Palin's Answer: "I'm not discouraged at all, even hearing those poll numbers because, for some reason, I have found myself over and over again in my life being put in these underdog positions and yet still when victory needed to be reached in order to meet the greater good, it's always worked out just perfectly fine despite the fact that over and over again...that I know that at the end of the day putting this in God's hands, that the right thing for America will be done, the end of the day on Nov. 4th"[167]

I guess the "right thing for America" this time was the election of Barack Obama.

9. Dinosaurs and People Coexisted

Palin told Mr. Munger, a local music teacher, that "dinosaurs and humans walked the Earth at the same time." When Mr. Munger asked her about prehistoric fossils and tracks dating back millions of years, Palin said, "she had seen pictures of human footprints inside the tracks."[168]

Matt Damon made a video posted on You Tube, wherein he explains that he really wants to know if she thinks dinosaurs were here 4000 years ago because…she's gonna have the nuclear codes.[169] "It's like a really bad Disney movie." "It's absurd, and I don't understand why more people aren't talking about it." … It's a terrifying possibility."[170]

10. United States Supreme Court Cases

Question: What other Supreme Court decisions (beside <u>Roe v. Wade</u>) do you disagree with?

Palin's Answer: " Well, let's see. There's — of course — in the great history of America rulings there have been rulings, that's never going to be absolute consensus by every American. And there are — those issues, again, like <u>Roe v. Wade</u> where I believe are best held on a state level and addressed there. So you know — going through the history of America, there would be others but …"

Question: Can you think of any?

Palin's Answer: "Well, I could think of — of any again, that could be best dealt with on a more local level. Maybe I would take issue with. But you know, as mayor, and then as governor and even as a Vice-President, if I'm so privileged to serve, wouldn't be in a position of changing those things but in supporting the law of the land as it reads today."[171]

11. Motivation to go into Politics

Question: What got you involved in politics?

Palin's Answer: "...and then I realized to be really able to make a difference-not just being one of six of a body but to make a difference-I would have to run for the top dog position, and so I ran for mayor...that there were changes, positive changes, that had to be ushered into our state government, decided to run for governor and do so, was successful, and here we are."[172]

I guess Governor Palin had made all the positive changes Alaska needed, so there was no reason to continue as Governor? Or was the problem as Levi Johnston described it that she indicated that she wondered why she took the job as Governor? Was it just too hard and there was too much going on?[173]

12. The Bailout Bill

Question: The House of Representative this week passed a bill, a big bailout bill—or didn't pass it, I should say. The Senate decided to pass it, and the House is wrestling with it still tonight. As America watches these things happen on Capitol Hill...was this the worst of Washington or the best of Washington...?

Palin's Answer: "...You know, I think a good barometer here, as we try to figure out has this been a good time or a bad time in America's economy, is go to a kid's soccer game on Saturday, and turn to any parent there on the sideline and ask them, "How are you feeling about the economy?"[174]

13. Spending

Question: (With regard to the subprime lending meltdown) Who do you think was at fault?

Palin's Answer: "…Let's do what our parents told us before we probably even got that first credit card. Don't live outside of our means."[175]

Would the debt Sarah left for the people in the small town of Wasilla of $1,675,000.00 qualify as "living outside our means"?

14. Homosexuality

Question: Do you support …granting same-sex benefits to couples?

Palin's Answer: "…if there's any kind of suggestion at all from my answer that I would be anything but tolerant of adults in "America choosing their partners, choosing relationships that they deem best for themselves, you know, I am tolerant…"[176]

Do you think Sarah Palin demonstrated this "TOLERANCE" when she sent the book "Daddy's Room-mate" to an outlying community of Wasilla?

15. The Importance of Education

"…America needs to be putting a lot more focus on that and our schools have got to be really ramped up in terms of funding that they are deserving. Teachers need to be paid more…."[177]

Does the example Sarah has set in her own home demonstrate her emphasis on the importance of education, or would she simply like her relatives (grandma, father, brother)[178] to be paid more? Certainly Sarah's kids, and her husband, don't seem to have internalized the importance of higher education.

16. Job of the Vice President

Question: "Governor you said in July that someone would have to explain to you exactly what it is the Vice-President does every day…what is it you think the Vice-Presidency is worth now?"

Palin's Answer: "No, no. Of course, we know what the Vice-President does. And that's not only to preside over the Senate and will take that position very seriously also. I'm thankful the Constitution would allow a bit more authority given to the Vice-President if that Vice-President so chose to exert it in working with the Senate and making sure that we are supportive of the President's policies and making sure too that our President understands what our strengths are. John McCain and I have had good conversations about where I would lead with his agenda…."[179]

Does Sarah think that her job would be to run the Senate? Is she saying that her job is to lead the Senate, and to make sure the Senate follows the President's agenda?

17. Sarah the Champion of All Children but Especially "Special Needs Children"

"…But it wasn't just that experience tapped into, it was my connection to the heartland of America. Being a mom, one very concerned about a son in the war, about a special needs child, about kids heading off to college…"[180]

What children of Sarah's are "heading off to college"? Is the special needs child the one she calls the "retarded one"?[181]

18. The Importance of Family to Sarah Palin.

When Sarah became Governor of Alaska, she had to move to Juneau. Todd refused to move, but made Bristol move to Juneau, even though Bristol wanted to stay in Wasilla to see Levi.[182] When the next school year began, Todd and Sarah tried to get Bristol to go back to Juneau, but she told them she wouldn't do it. She told them she wouldn't do it, and if they made her move there she was going to elope and move in with Levi. [183]

Instead her parents made her live with Heather, Sarah's sister in Anchorage. After the move to Anchorage, Bristol would have to drive 45 minutes to Levi's house if she wanted to see him.[184] Bristol became pregnant with Levi's child after that.

After Sarah's grandchild, Tripp, was born, she reportedly paid more attention to him than she did to Trig, her own Down-Syndrome child, the one she called "the retarded one."[185] On a typical day she reportedly would come home and tell Bristol that she was too tired to take care of her own baby, and Sarah would proceed to hibernate in her room until the next day started.[186]

Todd regularly appeared standing behind Sarah Palin at rallies, when cameras were running. However after the nomination of Mrs. Palin, the father of Sarah's grandson reported that Sarah and Todd wouldn't go anywhere together unless the cameras were out. Once the cameras were gone, they didn't talk to each other, unless they were fighting.[187] Levi never saw them sleep in the same room, even during the Republican Convention.[188]

After the Republican Convention the kids went back to Alaska. Sarah went off campaigning. It was about a month before she returned to Alaska for a visit.[189] Maybe this absence didn't matter to Sarah because even when she was living in Alaska, there reportedly "wasn't much parenting in that house."[190]

19. Abortion and Abstinence

It's no secret that Sarah Palin is against abortion, even in cases of rape or incest.[191] In fact she explains that even if her own daughter was the victim of rape that she would "choose life."[192] In fact Sarah explained: "I've always had near and dear to my heart the mission of protecting the sanctity of life and being pro-life, a hardcore pro-lifer, but I think this opportunity for me to really be walking the walk and not just talking the talk. …I feel so privileged and blessed to have been, I guess, chosen to have Trig enter our lives…"[193]

However, the only person to comment on Sarah's involvement in the life of that "special needs child" is Levi Johnson. Levi explained that Sarah calls the "special needs child" "the retarded one," and that she doesn't provide much, if any, care for this child.[194]

The amazing thing is that in spite of her rhetoric, Ms. Palin admits that she considered her choice when she learned that Trig would have Downs-Syndrome.[195]

Governor Palin has also advocated teaching "abstinence only" to teenage girls.[196] As referenced above, it appears Sarah Palin wasn't able to follow this "abstinence only" policy before she was married to Todd, and her own daughter who has had a child out of wedlock has stated that "abstinence for all teens is not realistic."[197] Sarah's position on "abstinence only" teaching is particularly troubling in light of the fact that Alaska saw the nation's biggest increase in teenage pregnancy rates from 2005 to 2006.[198]

20. Quitting

Sarah Palin, dressed in fishing gear, explained after her resignation as Governor of Alaska, that she was "NOT A QUITTER," she was a "fighter"[199]

However even reporters in Alaska, explained that "You don't prove you're a fighter by quitting."[200] You don't lead by taking a seat on the bench. You don't advance the game, or change the game, or even influence the game by getting out of the game.[201]

Chapter 4

Sarah Palin is NOT a Feminist

During the Katie Couric interview, Sarah stated that she thought of herself as a "Feminist."[202] My impression of a "Feminist" encompasses many things and many people, but Sarah Palin is not one of them. Even though I am a stay-at-home mom, I consider myself a Feminist. I consider Barack Obama a Feminist. Like Eve Ensler, I am a Feminist who is committed to trying to build community, help empower women and stop violence against them. That is why it is so offensive that Sarah Palin calls herself a Feminist. John McCain's choice of Sarah Palin to get the "women's vote" is insidious and cynical.[203] The critical consideration to assess whether any particular person is a Feminist is not their gender, whether they "say they are a Feminist, their status as a Governor, Senator, President, or a stay-at-home-mom. The critical consideration is whether the person respects women and considers women equal to men? Does the person seek to empower women and prevent them from becoming dependent upon anyone? Do they seek to prevent men from passing judgment on the worth of a woman? Certainly Governor Palin's own experience with her marriage to the father of her first-born,[204] her attitude towards her own daughter suggesting that she will have to marry Levi Johnston,[205] and her unwillingness to teach anything but abstinence would not indicate an interest in preventing women from becoming dependent upon others. Sarah Palin allowed men to judge her in the Miss Wasilla beauty pageant. She seems to think that a woman should not be given a choice regarding whether to give birth to the child of her rapist, even if the "CHOICE" is made days after the crime. She doesn't seem to find any problem with her 17 year old daughter becoming dependent upon her parents indefinitely. Education is the single most important thing a woman can do to ensure that she eliminates the possibility of becoming dependent upon any person. Bristol Palin has relinquished the dream of a college education, because she wasn't willing, or able, to follow the teaching of "abstinence only."

Barack Obama is a Feminist

President Obama wrote a letter to Malia and Sasha, describing why he ran for President of the United States. He explained…

> "…These are the things I want for you—to grow up in a world with no limits on your dreams and no achievements beyond your reach, and to grow into compassionate, committed women who will help build that world. And I want every child to have the same chances to learn and dream and grow and thrive that you girls have…."[206]

When I read this letter I cried. I felt as if the President of the United States was writing this letter to me, to my children, and to every citizen of the country. It was especially moving because it was written to his girls, and he referred to every "child" in the country instead of every boy or girl. Suddenly I understood the reason that, politics aside, Barack Obama is different from other leaders who have held the highest office in the land. The same equality that women have been advocating for over a century was now being advocated by our President. The President just happened to be an African American male. Even after the election, President Obama has recognized the importance and sacrifices women often make explaining that "The truth is that Michelle still had to make sacrifices of the sort that I did not have to make."[207]

In 1963 Betty Friedan published the historical book the *Feminine Mystique*.[208] Her book "...changed the consciousness of a country...and the world." Just three years after I left the practice of law, in April of 1997, Betty Friedan amended the text of The Feminine Mystique by adding an introduction entitled "Metamorphosis Two Generations Later.[209] Prophetically, she explained:

> "As we approach a new century—and a new millennium—it's the **men** who have to break through to a new way of thinking about themselves and society."

> "We may now begin to glimpse the new human possibilities when women and men are finally free to be themselves, know each other for who they really are, and define the terms and measures of success, failure, joy, triumph, power, and the common good together."[210]

Betty Friedan was the American feminist known for initiating the "second wave" of the Woman's Movement.[211] Born in 1921,[212] just one year after the ratification of the 19th Amendment, Betty Friedan was just a baby when Alice Paul and the Silent Sentinels were part of the "First Wave" of the feminist movement.[213] Ms. Friedan and Gloria Steinem were the primary founders of the National Organization for Women ("NOW") in 1966.[214] In 1970, the fiftieth anniversary of the ratification of the 19th Amendment, Ms. Friedan organized a nation-wide Women's Strike for Equality.[215] The strike resulted in unprecedented attention to the efforts of women to gain respect and attain their civil rights.[216] In New York City alone, over 50,000 women demonstrated;

Ms. Friedan died in 2006. She didn't live to witness the election of Barack Obama in 2008. I hope she heard his speech at the Democratic Convention in 2004? Without personally observing the historic election of 2008, she knew that the leader of the third wave of the Women's Movement would be a man.[217] She would be proud of our choice, and even prouder of the strength of the women who made it happen.

Is there any doubt about what Betty Friedan might think of Sarah Palin? I feel confident Betty Friedan would NOT consider Sarah a Feminist due to Sarah's position on (1) whether a woman should have a choice regarding an unwanted pregnancy in the case of rape or incest,[218] (2) whether a woman should have to pay for her own rape examination kit, which might cost $1000.00,[219] (3) whether teenage girls should be exposed to information regarding birth control instead of "abstinence only."[220] Maybe Sarah is a Rogue? Maybe Betty Friedan would consider Sarah to be a "scoundrel"? I am glad that Betty Friedan never heard Sarah Palin refer to herself as a "Feminist."

The third and final wave of the Women's Movement is here. Without calling Barack Obama a "Feminist," the women of this great country elected him as our leader. Before we analyzed his politics, and his positions on various economic and social issues, we determined that Barack Obama respects all people, regardless of *what* they are, and instead evaluates people for *who* they are. All 35,900,000 women who voted for Barack Obama are experiencing the excitement,

[221]

the thrill, and the satisfaction of riding the third wave with him. One day history books may describe the power and force of our voices in the election of 2008 as a tsunami.

Historical Perspective

The history of dissimilar treatment of women in our country is undisputed. Fortunately, women have been primarily our advocates, instead of our adversaries. Fortunately, Sarah Palin wasn't born until 1964.[222] By the time Sarah reached adulthood, women had already made great strides towards equal rights, so it was more difficult for Sarah Palin to have a significant impact on the image of women. However, even though many women have achieved national recognition for their intelligence, accomplishments, and their contributions to the American way of life, our battle is not over. Because Sarah Palin doesn't share many of the same attitudes of many women in our country, her nomination as John McCain's running mate was difficult for many of us. The women who had fought so diligently to establish the credibility of women were especially troubled by Sarah Palin. Perhaps Sarah is too young to appreciate the struggle of women who came before her. Perhaps she needs a refresher course in the liberation of women.

1. In 1776 Thomas Jefferson authored the Declaration of Independence, the most important document in U.S. history.[223] It prophetically declares:

> "We hold these truths to be self-evident, that all men are created equal, that they are endowed by their Creator with certain unalienable rights."[224]

What Tom really meant was that God must be a Caucasian, white, heterosexual man, and only those like himself, should be entitled to enjoy the rights of Life, Liberty, and the Pursuit of Happiness." He also assumed that God was not sexually attracted to women of another race, and certainly not to another man. For over 200 years civil rights leaders have been trying to dispel the notion that Thomas Jefferson was a racist, sexist, homophobe, and that he was simply not "politically correct" in his wording of the U.S. Constitution. The wisdom of the words "all men are created equal" has stood the test of time. However today we would substitute the language that, "all **people** are created equal." We should never take for granted the dedication of women, Blacks, and homosexuals to reach our current place in history.

2. In 1848 at Seneca Falls, New York, Elizabeth Cady Stanton and Lucretia Mott led the first women's rights convention.[225] This convention approved a document referred to as the "Declaration of Sentiments," which proclaimed that "all men and women were created equal"[226]… (70 years after the Declaration of Independence). Both men and women attended this convention protesting the mistreatment of women in social, economic, political, and religious life.

Elizabeth Cady Stanton and
Lucretia Mott, 1848 [227]

3. In 1873 Susan B. Anthony gave a memorable speech. She had been arrested for casting her vote for president, which was deemed to be "illegal."[228] In advocating the right of women to vote, she asserted:

> "Friends and fellow citizens: I stand before you tonight under indictment for the alleged crime of having voted at the last presidential election, without having a lawful right to vote. It shall be my work this evening to prove to you that in thus voting, I not only committed no crime, but instead, simply exercised my citizen's rights, guaranteed to me and all United States citizens by the National Constitution, beyond the power of any state to deny."[229]

She explained:

> "It was we, the people; not we, the white male citizens...Webster, Wordester, and Bouvier all define a citizen to be a person in the United States, entitled to vote and hold office. The only question left to be settled now is: Are we women persons?..."[230]

4. March 3, 1913 was the date of the first Suffragist Parade, held in Washington DC.[231] Thousands of people turned out to support the fight to grant voting rights to women.

The American Suffrage Campaign Parade [232]

5. In 1920, after greater than one year of protesting by the Silent Sentinels in front of the White House, after heroic effort by the National Women's Party, and after Alice Paul's hunger strike and the abuse that followed by her prison guards,[233] the 19th Amendment was finally ratified. It provides:

> "The right of citizens of the United States to vote shall not be denied or abridged by the United States or any State on account of sex…"[234]

Thus, it had taken our country fifty years longer to recognize a woman's right to vote, as compared to the right of a Black man to vote.

Landmark events in our struggle to achieve equality, even after the ratification of the 19th Amendment include:

- 1950—Harvard Law School admits a woman.

- 1950—The U.S. Census Bureau recognizes a woman's right to continue to use her maiden name after marriage.

- 1955—Rosa Parks refuses to give up her seat on the bus to a Caucasian man, resulting in her arrest and the Montgomery bus boycott.

- 1961—Eleanor Roosevelt chairs JFK's Commission on the Status of Women.

- 1961—"Women Strike for Peace" stage a one-day strike to further their cause, "End the Arms Race, Not the Human Race."

- 1963—Betty Friedan publishes *The Feminine Mystique.*

- 1965—In <u>Griswold v. State of Connecticut</u>, 381 U.S. 479 (1965), the Supreme Court rules that laws prohibiting use of birth control are unconstitutional.

- 1966—Betty Friedan, Gloria Steinem, and others attend the Third National Conference of the Commission on the Status of Women, and establish the National Organization for Women (NOW).

- 1966—Indira Gandhi , having won the leadership of the Congress Party, becomes the first female Prime Minister of India.

- 1967—Muriel Siebert becomes the first woman to own a seat on the New York Stock Exchange.

- 1969—Golda Meir becomes the first female Prime Minister of Israel.

- 1970—Anna Mae McCabe Hays becomes the first woman General in the U.S. Army.

- 1970—The debut of the Mary Tyler Moore Show. This show was a television breakthrough, with the first never-married, independent, professional, woman as the main character. Mary was not widowed, divorced, and she was not looking for a man who might support her. She was comfortable in her own skin.[235]

- 1971—The National Women's Political Caucus (NWPC) is founded by Gloria Steinem, Betty Friedan, and Bella Abzug.

- 1972—Ms. Magazine was founded.

- 1972—Shirley Chisholm becomes the first African American woman to run for president.

- 1973—Billie Jean King defeats champion Bobby Riggs in the "Battle of the Sexes."

- In Roe v. Wade, 410 U.S. 113 (1973), the United States Supreme Court ruled in 1973 that a woman has the right to terminate a pregnancy for any reason up until the fetus reaches viability.[236] In essence the Court found that the mother's rights were superior to those of a fetus, if the fetus could not survive on its own. Once the fetus reaches viability (i.e. it is no longer dependent upon the mother for survival), then additional considerations are to be factored into the decision, and the mother's rights are then limited by the interest of the unborn child. The Court based the decision upon the Right of Privacy in the U.S. Constitution.[237]

- 1975—In Taylor v. Louisiana, 419 U.S. 522 (1975) the U.S. Supreme Court rules, for the first time, that women can't be excluded from juries based upon their gender.

- 1978—The Pregnancy Discrimination Act is passed.

- 1979—Margaret Thatcher becomes the first female Prime Minister of the United Kingdom.

- 1981—Collaboration between Georgeanna Jones and Howard Jones results in the conception of the first in-vitro fertilization in the U.S.

- 1981—Sandra Day O'Connor becomes the first woman appointed to the U.S. Supreme Court.

- 1982— Brenda Berkman begins her career as a New York City firefighter after winning a federal sex discrimination lawsuit.

- 1983—Barbara McClintock wins the Nobel Prize in Physiology or Medicine.

- 1986—The U.S. Supreme Court rules in Meritor Savings Bank v. Vinson, 477 U.S. 57 (1986) that sexual harassment is a violation of Title VII of the Civil Rights Act.

- 1986—Rita Levi-Montalcini and Stanley Cohen are awarded the Nobel Prize in Physiology or Medicine for their discoveries pertaining to nerve growth.

- 1988—Gertrude Elion wins the Nobel Prize for the treatment of childhood leukemia, the herpes virus, immune disorders, arthritis, and other diseases.

- 1989—Wendy Wasserstein wins the Pulitzer Prize for *The Heidi Chronicles.*

- 1990—Darlene Iskra becomes the first female commander of a U.S. Navy ship.

- 1992—Mae Jemison becomes the first African American woman to go into space.

- 1993—Ruth Bader Ginsburg becomes the second female Justice on the United States Supreme Court.

- 1993—Janet Reno becomes the first female U.S. attorney general.

- 1996—Taliban government places strict restrictions on women, forbidding them from receiving an education or working outside the home.

- 1996—A report from the World Health Organization urges the immediate ending of female genital mutilation, already performed on an estimated 100 million girls worldwide.

- 2001—Hillary Rodham Clinton who was the First Lady at the time, is elected as a Senator from New York.

- 2004—A Nigerian appeals court overturns the death sentence (by stoning) of Amina Lawal in an adultery case.

- 2005—Sandra Day O'Connor, having reached the pinnacle of success as an attorney, announces that she will resign from the United States Supreme Court after serving 24 years, to be with her husband who was in poor health. [238]

- 2005—Wangari Maathai, an environmental activist, becomes the first Black African woman to win the Nobel Peace Prize.

- 2006—Kuwaiti women are granted the right to vote.

- 2007—Nancy Pelosi becomes the first woman to serve as Speaker of the U.S. House of Representatives.

- The United States Supreme Court ruled in May of 2007, in the case of <u>Ledbetter v. Goodyear</u>, that it was permissible for an employer to discriminate against an employee, if the employee doesn't file suit within 180 days of the alleged discrimination.[239] Ms. Ledbetter, an employee of Goodyear Tire and Rubber Co. for almost 20 years, took early retirement and sued her previous employer, asserting that she received disparate pay over the course of her employment, and that this difference in pay was the result of intentionally discriminatory acts. In a 5-4 decision, the Supreme Court ruled that the relevant statute was constitutional, and that Ms. Ledbetter was not allowed to complain about any differences in pay unless they occurred within the 180 days before filing suit. She was prohibited from recovering damages for any harm that had occurred more than 180 days before the filing of suit. This decision was particularly offensive because Ms. Ledbetter didn't know of the discrimination until after she retired. In essence, the Court indicated that it was permissible for an employer to discriminate, so long as the employer is clever and hides the discrimination for at least 180 days, preventing the woman from bringing suit within the statutory period.[240]There was a strong dissent in the <u>Ledbetter</u> case, written by Justice Ginsburg, a woman. She was joined in her dissent by three other Justices. She argued that the application of the 180 day rule was not appropriate because pay discrimination often occurs in small increments over large periods of time.[241] Never-the-less the majority of the Court ruled against Ms. Ledbetter. John McCain agreed with the Court's decision. Barack Obama did not.

- 2008—General Ann Dunwoody becomes the first woman to serve as a four-star general in the U.S. Army.

- 2008—Barack Obama is elected the 44th President. The *"third wave"* of the American Feminist Movement gains a new leader.[242]

- 2009—Michelle Obama becomes the first African American to be the First Lady.[243]

- 2009—Barack Obama creates the Council on Women and Girls, and appoints Valerie Jarrett as its leader.[244]

- 2009—Barack Obama signs his first bill, as President of the United States, the Lilly Ledbetter Fair Pay Restoration Act.[245]

- 2009—Barack Obama nominates Judge Sonia Sotomayor to the U.S. Supreme Court.[246] Judge Sotomayor graduated summa cum laude from Princeton University and became the editor of the Law Journal at Yale Law School.[247] Over her three-decade career, she has served in a wide variety of legal roles, including prosecutor, litigator, and judge on the Second Circuit Court of Appeals in New York.[248] Judge Sotomayor's mother was a single mom from the time her daughter was 9 years old, often working two jobs to support the family.[249] Judge Sotomayor stated:

"My mother has devoted her life to my brother and me. And as the President mentioned, she worked often two jobs to help support us after dad died. I have often said that I am all I am because of her, and I am only half the woman she is."[250]

- 2009—The Obama administration offers several new educational benefits that directly benefit mothers, including National Pell Grants, Tuition Tax credits, and Comprehensive improvements to the Federal Family Education Loan Program.[251] While these programs benefit both men and women, women benefit from these programs to a greater degree. Women are more likely than men to participate in an educational activity(49% women, 43% men)[252] and many of these programs target on-line degrees which are ideal for stay-at-home mothers.[253]

- 2009—The Senate approves the nomination of Judge Sonia Sotomayor as the 111th Justice of the United States Supreme Court. She is the first Latina to serve on the Court, and only the third woman.[254]All 31 votes against her confirmation were from Republicans. [255] Two of the nine Republicans who voted to confirm her nomination were female, Susan Collins of Maine, and Olympia Snowe, also of Maine.[256]

- 2009—President Obama awards the Presidential Medal of Freedom, the highest civilian honor a president may award, to Justice Sandra Day O'Connor.[257]

- 2009— President Obama awarded the Medal of Freedom to:

Nancy Goodman Brinker, the founder of the Susan G. Komen, Race for the Cure foundation, as the champion in the fight against breast cancer.

Billie Jean King for her work since her victory over Bobby Riggs in the "Battle of the Sexes" fighting for gender equality.

Chita Rivera for her accomplishments as the first Hispanic woman to win life-time achievement awards in the performing arts.

Mary Robinson for her role as the first female president of Ireland.

It has been 140 years since the enactment of the 15th Amendment, and over 200 years since the signing of the Declaration of Independence. Almost a century has passed since women won the right to vote. Time does heal. We as a country learned tolerance and understanding. Barack Obama was our teacher, and we the students. He was a powerful teacher, and we were dedicated students. Some may not yet have learned this lesson, but unquestionably, those students are now part of the minority in America. Whatever events may be in our future, the majority of Americans have let their voices join in a resounding chorus, shouting to the entire world a new verse: **The Majority of Americans will No Longer Tolerate Racism!** We might follow that first verse with this second verse: **The Majority of American Women have the Wisdom to Disregard Gender!** Even though Sarah Palin calls herself a Feminist, the women of America determined that she is not.

Women proved that we do in fact disregard gender when making our decisions regarding the person who will earn our vote. We did not elect Sarah as our Vice-President. Given Palin's limited experience, limited education, limited knowledge of history, limited knowledge of geography, limited knowledge of the fossil records, McCain must have been focused upon gender. McCain's choice of Sarah Palin as his running mate vividly illustrates his standards for judging a woman, and his standards are not attractive.

Chapter 5

Shame on you, John McCain!

John McCain exercised very poor judgment, or no judgment at all, when he selected Sarah Palin. By selecting Sarah Palin, Senator McCain demonstrated that winning an election was more important to him than the security of our country. Given his age and medical history, John should have put a significant amount of time, effort, energy, and thought into the selection of a Vice-President. Even if Sarah Palin was unable to appreciate how ill prepared she was to serve as Vice-President, John McCain knew better. To put Sarah Palin in a position that she could have been the President of the United States of America, was criminal. Even if you convince yourself that someone in the cabinet would make most of the critical decisions regarding the economy, the environment, constitutional law issues, Sarah Palin's judgment would have been the difference between a world at peace, and a nuclear holocaust. Why would anyone think that Sarah Palin had more judgment and insight about a nuclear war than she has about dinosaurs, and their co-existence with humans. Did John McCain think she would be more insightful when talking to Putin than she was during the interview with turkeys being slaughtered in the background. Do you think John McCain understood Sarah Palin when she answered questions during her single interview with him? Was there even a question and answer session in the interview, or just an assessment of her All-American face and form? Shame on you John McCain for having so little regard for the future of this country.

How did this happen? How could a U.S. Senator evaluating any candidate for the position of Vice-President think that Sarah Palin was fit to lead, unless the single criterion was appearance? Maybe John's age was more of a factor than we thought. John McCain was born in 1936.[258] My mother was just two years old when John was born. John jokes that he is "older than dirt" and he admits he doesn't use a computer.[259] During John's life, men and women have learned to ride all three waves of Feminism, and he failed to notice. John never learned to surf. John did notice men and women in the ocean. He didn't pay much attention to the men, and all he noticed about the women was their "All-American form." Maybe that is why he chose a swim-suit model for his first wife.[260] He failed to notice that those women he was watching were surfing one of three waves. He totally missed the fact that some of us had perfected our skills, allowing us to jump from one wave to another. Perhaps he can join my mom on a cruise ship, and she can point out those who have mastered the art of surfing. If he looks carefully among those riding the third wave he might even recognize one of his adversaries, Barack Obama.

Mrs. "Uncle Sam"

My first thought was… "Well Shit!" It was 3:00 p.m., and the competition had arrived. No one had been out campaigning for McCain all day. Among the mosaic of campaign signs that adorned the polling pace for our precinct, there wasn't a single McCain sign. The many signs at the polling place punctuated the fact that it was Election Day, and this was the polling place for precinct 1119. Lynn had been out holding his "Obama" sign at our designated polling place for the last three hours. Uncle Sam would have thought Lynn was his twin brother. His full, snow-white beard encircled the lower half of his face. Everything about his attire was red, white, or blue. The towering patriotic hat hid his bald head. The red and white stripes of his pants accentuated his stature. A blue jacket and white shirt dignified the ensemble, making him appear only half like he was wearing a costume. In this outfit, while holding an Obama sign, Lynn was the perfect person to attract the attention of passers-bye, reminding them that it was Nov. 4th, and if they had not yet voted for Barack Obama for President, today was the day.

Lynn, as Uncle Sam
Dallas Texas, Nov. 4, 2008,
Polling Place, Precinct 1119.

Now another person was going to compete for attention from voters. This "other person" was a female, dressed in a patriotic outfit, as if she were "Mrs. Sam." It was surprising to me that she would appear publically in the outfit that so tightly clung to her many curves. Had she been dressed in jeans and a sweatshirt, as I was, her figure would not have attracted any attention. She was only modestly over-weight, so her physique would not have been hard on the eye, but-for her tight-fitting, brightly colored clothes. Because her red and white shorts shared the same panty lines as her underpants, her robust thighs reminded me of something only seen on the midway at the Texas State Fair. "Well endowed" is the way a polite woman would describe the bosoms that spilled out of the blue tuxedo style jacket, with tails so long that they extended to the top of her red-patent leather, Nancy Sinatra-style go-go boots. The only thing that could add the perfect compliment to this impressive menagerie of components, was the bleach-blond brittle hair of this woman that hung from her top hat. This bright yellow filament, erupting from her head, screamed at the people driving past… "If you like what you see, vote for John McCain." Some men acknowledged her, honking as they passed by.

The polling place was open until 7:00 p.m. I had been sitting next to my Suburban for eleven hours, and had another hour left before the polling place closed. Fortunately, Mrs. Sam left around dusk. I guess she thought her two hours of "work" for the McCain campaign was enough. Some might argue that the 5 ft. x 5 ft. sign on the back of my Suburban was excessive, or that the window paint on the windows proclaiming… "Yes, we can!!!" was over the top. Yet to me they seemed small in comparison to the woman in the Mrs. Sam outfit. I prided myself on the quiet demeanor I showed by simply holding the Obama sign, and not yelling at people as they passed by. My "outfit" in contrast, included jeans, tennis shoes, a jacket, and grey sweat-shirt advertising "Obama 08" in red, white, and blue, in very small conservative letters, in the upper left corner.

Mrs. Sam's appearance at the polling place really bothered me. I assumed, at the time, that it was just the fact that she was campaigning for McCain. In retrospect, Mrs. Sam was the epitome of all that the McCain campaign stood for, and the type of women that I associated with his campaign. I will be the first to acknowledge that there are impressive, educated, Republican women. However, most of those women have little in common with John McCain. I have no way of knowing if Mrs. Sam was an educated woman, but she hid it well if she were. I have no way of knowing her attitude about men, and whether she was a woman who demanded respect from men, but the honks she provoked did not leave the impression she was standing on the curb to impress passers-bye with her intellect.

John McCain's Attitude Toward Women

As I reflect on the entire campaign of John McCain, Mrs. Sam was the perfect example of the McCain campaign. She was the opposite of the multitude of women that I met who were working for the Obama campaign. From my work at the Dallas office, work at voter registration events, working in Ohio, caucusing during the primary, and in the many meetings I attended as part of the campaign effort, never did I see a woman who looked as tacky as Mrs. Sam. Madeleine Albright explained my feelings quite well. Madeline Albright, the first female Secretary of State, and a college professor at Georgetown University, was quoted as saying:

> "The truth is, if you care about the status of women in our society, and in our troubled economy, the best choice by far in this election is Obama-Biden"[261]

I don't think Mrs. Sam worried too much about the status of women in our society, when she stood on the curb in her outfit waving at men as they passed by and honked.

John McCain is an example to all the world of an attitude toward women that most women, and especially educated women, will not tolerate. From his attitude toward his wives, to his attitude toward choosing a Vice-Presidential candidate, John McCain's has consistently conveyed his lack of respect for women.[262] He used Cindy to gain public recognition and wealth. Cindy McCain may tolerate his attitude, but we won't! He used Sarah Palin to attempt to gain the votes of women. Sarah may not have blinked, but we are blinking as fast as we can. In November of 2008 women cried out, and we were heard. The chorus of our voices was deafening. We are just now learning the lyrics, but the passion we felt was shared by all the women who worked and voted for Barack Obama. Only time will tell whether the next candidates will heed our voices.

John McCain, the Senator, and war hero, became the Republican Party's presumptive nominee for President in early March 2008.[263] Forget his age, his medical history, his involvement in the Keating Five[264], or his stance on many issues that women might find intolerable (not the least of which was his agreement with the Supreme Court's ruling in Ledbetter v. Goodyear[265]). Let's consider his personal history with women, and the respect, or lack thereof, which he demonstrated.

For his first wife he chose Carol Shepp. Although not a beauty queen, she was a swim suit model, born in 1937, just a year after John.[266] They were married in July of 1965.[267] By the summer of 1967 he was involved in combat duty.[268] By October of 1967 he was taken as prisoner of war and was not released until March of 1973, five years later.[269] Thus, before active duty and being taken prisoner of war, he had only been married to his first wife for about two years. During his imprisonment Carol became very active in the POW/MIA movement.[270] When he returned from being a POW, he found his wife had been involved in a serious car accident in December of 1969.[271] She had been in the hospital for six months, and underwent 23 surgical procedures.[272] The car accident left her crippled.[273] Carol was no longer the woman that magazines would feature as a swim suit model, and she was not able to generate significant monetary contributions to the family budget.

Within three years after his release from prison, John McCain was admittedly having extra-marital affairs.[274] In April of 1979 he met Cindy Lou Hensley, a rodeo queen, and an heiress to a family fortune.[275] Cindy was 25 years old, and poor Carol was now 42 and crippled.[276] John was 43 and looking for an easy way to improve his position in life. John capitalized on this opportunity to trade up. If he divorced Carol and married Cindy he would get a beauty queen and money. It didn't take him long to figure this one out. By March of 1980, less than a year after meeting Cindy, John McCain was divorced.[277] Within two months, by May 1980, John McCain was married to Cindy Lou.[278] Within about one year after his marriage to Cindy, John McCain retired from the Navy, moved to Arizona where his wealthy and influential father-in-law lived.[279] John became employed by his wealthy father-in-law, and by 1982 he was a member of the U.S. House of Representatives.[280] Thus in the span of three years, he had divorced his crippled wife, married a wealthy beauty queen who was 18 years younger, and used her family money to ensure his election as Arizona's Representative in the U.S. House. He is not my hero.

Did John love Cindy? Maybe. But whatever their personal relationship, the appearance created by John was that he used Cindy to help him achieve political success. It appears that his goal was not to use her intellect, but to take advantage of her money and the appearance of success since she was a "pretty wife." Even in the campaign of 2008, Cindy was usually seen, not heard, standing behind John, but looking pretty and much younger than McCain. It appeared that this was John's idea of the appropriate role for women..."trim." Beauty Queens have a lot of experience looking pretty and not saying anything. Their purpose is to look pretty, but not to speak. Maybe Cindy had something to say and John just forgot to ask.

Perhaps the most telling story about John McCain's attitude toward Cindy, and towards women in general, was reported in *The Real McCain*, by Cliff Schecter:

> "Three reporters from Arizona, on the condition of ano-nymity, also let me in on another incident involving McCain's intemperateness. In his 1992 Senate bid, McCain was joined on the campaign trail by his wife, Cindy, as well as campaign aide Doug Cole and consul-tant Wes Gullett. At one point, Cindy playfully twirled McCain's hair and said, "You're getting a little thin up there." McCain's face reddened, and he responded, "At least I don't plaster on the makeup like a trollop, you cunt."[281]

It is interesting to note that McCain had a person ask about this incident at a campaign stop. McCain refused to answer the person who asked him about this incident.[282] Of course we cared! Of course we would ask questions!?! Of course, we would like to get answers! Describing his beautiful wife, whose wealth secured his political success, with such hostility, is a vivid exam-ple of the disrespect and contempt McCain must have for women. If he refers to his wife this way in public places, how does he refer to female Senators?

McCain has a history of disrespecting women. Consider the joke he told in a public forum, before the National League of Cities and Towns in Washington D.C.:

> "...(have you heard the one about a ...) woman who is attacked on the street by a gorilla, beaten senseless, raped repeatedly, and left to die?....
>
> When she finally regains consciousness and tries to speak, her doctor leans over to hear her sigh contently and to feebly ask, "where is that marvelous ape?"[283]

This joke could only be amusing if: (1) you find rape entertaining, (2) you consider the beating of a woman funny, and (3) you agree with the point of the joke that a woman's idea of a meaningful sexual experience is to be repeatedly raped! John must have thought that this was a funny joke or why would he tell it at all? What does he convey to all women in the audience? John should at least pretend to respect women! If he tells this type of joke in public, what does he share with male friends, behind closed doors?

When he decided that he needed to get the "woman's vote" in his bid for the 2008 presidential election, of course he assumed that the way to get the woman's vote would be to choose one of them. It must not have occurred to him that women might scrutinize the woman he chose, as they would any other candidate, regardless of sex, or sexual preference. Because his way of valuing a woman was to judge her appearance, a beauty queen had the credentials he sought.

The Evolution of Miss America

John McCain was born in 1936. Just a few years earlier, in 1921, the very first Miss America was crowned.[284] The contestants wore wool swim suits, with baggy tunic tops over leggings or bloomers.[285]

1921 Miss America Finalists[286]

Margaret Gorman, 16 years old, was awarded the coveted title of the first Miss America, in part because of her appearance in the swim suit, but also because she had the best potential to "shoulder the responsibilities of homemaking and motherhood."[287]

By 1928 the Miss America Pageant was discontinued due to charges of indecency by women's organizations which asserted

Margaret Gorman
1921 Miss America[288]

that the swim suits were too revealing.[289] In the 30's, the decade of John McCain's birth, the pageant was resumed.[290] So, for at least the first half of John McCain's life, the ultimate aspiration of many women, including myself until age 11, was to be Miss America. Bert Parks was known as the emcee for the pageant, and is remembered for his praise of women in this melodic tune:

"There she is, Miss America,
There she is, your ideal.
The dream of a million girls,
Who are more than pretty
Can come true in Atlantic City,
For she may turn out to be…
The queen of femininity!

There she is, Miss America
There she is, your ideal.
With so many beauties
She took the town by a storm
With her All-American face and form.

And there she is!
Walking on air she is!
Fairest of fair, she is!
Miss America.[291]

It wasn't until 1990 that there was even a section of the pageant devoted to an interview.[292] Thus for 60 years, it never occurred to anyone to ask any of the contestants in the pageant to speak. Why would we ask them to speak? Obviously, John McCain wouldn't advocate changing the rules to allow women to speak. The contest was not about anything but appearances, so why would the audience care what a contestant had to say? Implicit, in a "beauty contest," is the notion that the "winner" would be the most attractive, not the smartest. Funny that these contests were judged predominantly by men, and that even after the interview became a part of the contest, it did not merit the majority of the points awarded.[293] To my knowledge, there is no GPA requirement, or academic excellence required for any of the women who enter the contest. The judges do not see or ask for an academic transcript or resume. Admittedly, this is not a contest to find a "bright" pretty woman; it is to find the most beautiful. Thus John's choice of Sarah Palin was logical. If he wanted to pick a woman, he would logically look for the most beautiful that he could find. Thus, Sarah was a logical choice. She was a beauty pageant winner, and the mother of a lot of kids. Isn't that what women would find to be impressive?

A significant mockery has been made by comedians of the interview event in these beauty contests. Unfortunately, the most revealing script has been provided by one of the contestants herself. The most publicized interview of a beauty contestant might be the answer of Miss Carolina, while competing for the title of Miss Teen USA, 2007. The interview went something like this…

"Judge:

Q: Recent polls have shown 1/5 of American's can't locate America on a world map. Why do you think this is?

Miss South Carolina: (and this is exactly what she said)
A: "I personally believe that, U.S. Americans are unable to do so, because some… people out there in our nation that don't have maps, and I believe that our education, like such, as in South Africa and Iraq, everywhere like such as, and I believe that they should… our education over here in the U.S., should help the U.S., err, should help South Africa and should help the Iraq and the Asian countries so we will be able to build up our future.., for our…

Announcer: Thank you very much South Carolina"[294]

My daughters have never watched the Miss America Pageant, but they both could immediately direct me to the You-tube site of this answer by Miss South Carolina. Coincidentally, this answer by Miss South Carolina has been compared to the answers given by Sarah Palin in her interview with Katie Couric.[295] Many of the contestants in these pageants may be bright, educated women. Since we don't place much value on what they say, I guess the message is… "What you have to say isn't important. Just shut-up and let the male judges assess your All-American face and form?!"

At least John McCain acted consistently throughout the campaign. He rarely allowed Cindy to speak, and Palin was limited to canned speeches. McCain certainly didn't let Palin conduct town-hall type of meetings as he did, fielding questions from the crowd. Who knows what she might have said? In summary, John McCain assumed that all women today still think that their "dream come true" would be to be a beauty queen. He chose a wife who was 18 years his junior, a rich beauty queen. Logically when he decided it might be to his political advantage to chose a woman as his Vice-Presidential running mate, his focus was appearance, not substance. Even though he may not have understood why the woman's vote was important, certainly he gave them the recognition deserved. He married a rodeo queen, and chose one of their queens to be Vice-President. What more could women possibly want? If he had been elected, and something happened to him, wouldn't we want a beauty queen to take over and run the country? She would certainly "wow" all the leaders of foreign countries, assuming they were men. She would be the fairest of the fair, with her All-American face and form. Imagine if our next president was a smart, unattractive woman. The outrage…?!?

It seems only fitting that the Miss America pageant is now being held in Las Vegas.[296] Last time I checked, Nevada was one of only two states in the entire country where prostitution is legal.[297] Thus we can predict who might be the "target audience" for the Miss America Pageant today. Maybe John McCain's age was more of a factor in the election than we realized at the time. Maybe because of his age, his view of women was formed in the 30's and 40's when women in society were viewed quite differently. Does John McCain believe in evolution? Perhaps organizers for the Miss America pageant, upon John's retirement from politics, should invite him to be a judge. He seems to know a beauty queen when he sees one!

Chapter 6

The Women's Vote Was Critical

As early as June 16th of 2008, GALLUP polls predicted that Barack Obama would win the election in Nov. of 2008.[298] As early as June, Gallup Poll Daily Tracking showed Obama was favored by women over McCain, by 50% to 38%.[299] Men preferred McCain by a margin of 48% to 42%.[300] Even though men slightly favored Obama by November, the margin was very small. It was the women who made the difference. Barack Obama beat John McCain in the election of November of 2008 by a significant margin. Obama carried the popular vote by a 6% margin.[301] CNN reported that over 66 million voters cast their ballots for Obama, as compared to approximately 58 million votes for McCain.[302] It was estimated that 66% of Americans voted, which was the largest percentage since 1908.[303] The 2008 race produced an astonishing number of first-time voters. Approximately four million new voters cast their ballots in 2008, as compared to the 2004 presidential election.[304] The close race of 2004, between Kerry and Bush, gave Senator Obama a road map to victory. If he could win the electoral votes won by John Kerry in 2004, and convert just a couple of Bush states, he could win the election of 2008. Obama succeeded in winning all the Kerry-states, and he converted nine

"W" states.[305] Obama received 365 electoral votes, (only 270 were required to win), to McCain's 173 electoral votes.[306]

Barack Obama was elected as the 44th President of the United States![307] It was **women** who made the difference! In 2004 women voters made up 54% of all voters. Bush received only 48% of the women's vote.[308] Thus it was the men's vote that caused Bush to be elected for a second term. Women voters in the landmark victory of 2008 constituted 53% of all voters.[309] Experts estimate that 35,900,000 women voted for Obama, as compared to 27,800,000 men.[310] Women favored Obama over McCain by 13%.[311] While men favored Obama, it was only by 1%. The margin of victory was staggering among female voters. Fifty six percent of women who "reached for the ballot" cast their votes for Barack Obama.[312] Because women constituted 53% of the voters in the election of 2008, the outcome of this election could have been very different if we had voted for the ticket with the woman. Instead we cast our ballots for Barack Obama. Wouldn't we be hypocrites if we voted based upon gender, after complaining for over 100 years that gender should not be considered in decisions regarding hiring and firing, promotions, salary determinations, elections … or even who does the laundry.

Both Obama and McCain made a conscious effort to win the women's vote.[313] The approach of McCain was simplistic. McCain assumed, erroneously, that if he chose a woman as his Vice-Presidential running-mate, women would necessarily vote for him. McCain's choice of Sarah Palin was the epitome of tokenism.[314] In making the selection of Sarah Palin, McCain gave us a paint-by-number picture of his view of women.

Number 1: He picked a pretty woman, a beauty queen, as his running mate, indicating his standard for judging the worth of a woman.

Number 2: He indicated that qualifications, ethics, experience, knowledge of current events and basic world geography, or even an appreciation for the offensiveness of the slaughter of animals, were not important for a pretty woman to possess.

Number 3: Even though John must have known Sarah was not competent to lead, did he think she would simply take over as the figure head? John wasn't worried about what would happen to our country if Sarah became our leader. If that happened, he would be dead! Besides Sarah had a husband who could guide her! Todd doesn't have a college degree, but he has a Y chromosome, so ...not to worry.

Number 4: John McCain insulted the female voters of America by assuming that we were not capable of, or smart enough, to disregard gender and evaluate candidates based upon their qualifications. I have never been fond of paint-by- number pictures. I don't like the fact that someone thinks I am not smart enough to choose my own colors.

Mistakenly, John McCain assumed that women were only capable of identifying with the candidates' reproductive organs instead of her views on issues. Sorry to disappoint! Senator McCain must not have been privy to current statistics, indicating a growing trend in the number of female applicants to, and graduates of, colleges.[315] In June of 2007 the U.S. Census Bureau reported that 56% of college undergraduates were women and 59% of people pursuing advanced degrees were women.[316] Of course, how would he know this valuable information since he doesn't use a computer?[317] My mother is in her seventies, and she communicates by computer, daily. I guess John McCain wouldn't know that either. She wouldn't qualify as "trim," so he would have no reason to "talk" to her.

Someone must have told John McCain that women might make a difference in this election. Ignoring the fact that Palin didn't support many issues common to the majority of women, John sought her out. While his contact with her before the nomination was limited, only meeting with her one time,[318] he was confident that Sarah Palin would spark enthusiasm and attract votes. Certainly one meeting was more than enough to assess Sarah's physical appearance. Judges in beauty pageants complete their assessment in a fairly limited amount of time, and certainly John McCain is smarter than most judges in beauty pageants. Although there was an initial bump in the women's reaction to Palin, it was short lived. Within two weeks after the announcement of Palin as the Vice-Presidential choice by McCain, his popularity started a steep decline, that never recovered.[319]

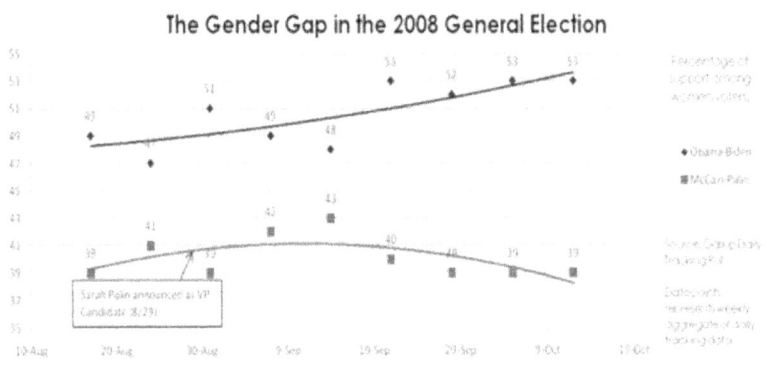

The Gender Gap in the 2008 General Election

320

Contrast McCain's approach to that of Senator Obama. Obama emphasized his support for pay equity and work/life balance policies.[321] While working for the Obama campaign in Ohio, one of the tasks I performed was to process flyers that would be sent to thousands of Ohio residents. One of the flyers emphasized the recent decision of the U.S. Supreme Court in the Ledbetter[322] case, and highlighted McCain's support of that decision.[323] The decision had the effect of denying equal pay to Lilly Ledbetter for her entire career at Goodyear. Obama also stressed McCain's votes against pay equity legislation and expanded health insurance for children.[324] Almost a year before the election, the New York Times reported on Dec. 1st, 2007, that the Obama campaign was trying to "turn years of Feminist thinking on its head and argue that the best candidate for women may, in fact, be a man. … Mr. Obama, like the rest of the field, has little choice but to compete for women's votes; 54 percent of Democratic caucus goers in Iowa four years ago were women, as were 54 percent of Democratic primary voters in New Hampshire."[325] What a novel concept, that the gender of a candidate should *not* be the reason to elect, or reject, him/her. How did Obama convince women that the best candidate for women might in fact be a man? Some of us didn't need convincing. However others needed a push. How did he inspire so many women to turn out the vote for him?

The portion of the Obama website, which specifically targeted women, featured different demographics of women. The first was Rebecca, a 48 year old mother of two daughters. Rebecca explained:

> "…This is the first political campaign I've been involved in, in my entire life, and I'm doing it for my daughters. I'm absolutely convinced that Barack is uniquely qualified to give my daughters a chance at a bright future because his ideas and his leadership address our 21st century challenges, both domestically and abroad."[326]

Lynn also told her story:

> "…I've never donated a penny to a political campaign before. …Never volunteered either. But as I'm getting older, I realize a lot of things are affecting my life right now.…I have a small business and I see how a lot of people with small business are struggling. And we can't afford to pay for health insurance ….We have to do something

ourselves. And I realized, if I don't do something, who will?"[327]

There was Nicole, the mother of 2-yr old Gavin and eight week old Hayden. Nicole is from Georgia. She explained her involvement:

"…I was struck by how thoughtful, composed, and straightforward he seemed. Our country is at a critical juncture. We have the opportunity to elect someone who is intelligent and thoughtful about the interests of our nation, and speaks to the dreams and aspirations of so many of us. Now is the time to get out and get involved. It's time to return honor and admiration to the United States' reputation in the world. It's time to create a moment where we can all make our country a better and more prosperous place. It's time to help Barack Obama."

In addition to volunteering, Nicole got her husband registered to vote.[328]

Finally, Hannah and Jonna, were volunteers from Vermont who were working in New Hampshire every weekend. Jonna inspired us:

"Hannah and I had never met before but went out together each weekend to canvass……The only thing that can defeat us now is complacency…"[329]

Each of these women, Rebecca, Lynn, Nicole, Hannah, and Jonna, were examples of the women who each made a difference in the campaign. The first three were women whose profiles were like thousands of other women who desperately wanted change. The last two were role models for all of us who were willing to do our part as volunteers. Additionally Nicole inspired her husband to register to vote, suggesting that women could inspire others, both men and women, to register, and later to vote. Portions of the stories of each of these women were similar to my story. Like Rebecca, I was doing my part in hopes that it would secure a better future for my children. Like Lynn, I had never before donated a penny to any political campaign. Like Nicole, I got a member of my family registered (my son Zach), knowing that if he did, he would ultimately cast his vote for Obama. Like Hannah and Jonna, I worked as often as I could to make a difference. Even though I didn't see this portion of the web-site until shortly before the election, I knew the story of each of these women before I heard it. It was my story. It is now our story. It was not Sarah Palin's story.

Without being privy to statistics regarding actual numbers of volunteers for the Obama campaign, my experience suggests that there were thousands of women volunteering. While there were unquestionably thousands of men who were essential to the campaign, the majority of volunteers at all events I attended were women. This is consistent with the general trend that women volunteer more than men for virtually all causes.[330]

Financial contributions of women were also significant. The Wall Street Journal reported that campaign finance data through July 31, 2008 showed that women had donated $109.5 million to the presidential campaigns for both candidates, Obama and McCain.[331] While men may have donated more to both McCain and Obama, women favored Obama in their campaign contributions, donating in excess of $50 million dollars to the Obama campaign.[332]

Statistics aside, why did women support Barack Obama? What was it that we saw and found so compelling? Pundits and political analysts would cite the many policies that Obama favored that were in line with the thinking of most women. But there was more. As wise, educated, and experienced women, who have been undervalued by men throughout history, what was it about this man that we found so compelling? When he spoke I had the feeling that he respected women as equals. I had the impression that he appreciated the sacrifices and contributions to his life that his mother, grandmother, and wife have made. When we look to his choice of wives, he didn't pick a woman who would qualify as "trim." He chose a life partner, who he respects, and who he considers the "rock" in his life.[333]

In his book, the Audacity of Hope, Barack explains....

" ... If there's one thing that social conservatives have been right about, it's that our modern culture sometimes fails to fully appreciate the extraordinary emotional and financial contributions—the sacrifices and just plain hard work—of the stay-at-home- mom."[334]

"It was the women, then, who provided the ballast in my life—my grandmother, whose dogged practicality kept the family afloat, and my mother, whose love and clarity of spirit kept my sister's and my world centered. Because of them I never wanted for anything important. From them I would absorb the values that guide me to this day."[335]

In my mind this is a man who understands the challenges of women, and who respects women. Barack Obama had the wisdom to treat the women in his life with respect. He was our candidate! He is our President.

In January of 2008, after a tough loss in the New Hampshire primary, Barack Obama announced that he was "still fired up and ready to go."[336] He proceeded to give his Yes We Can speech, and declared...

"...It was a creed written into the founding documents that declared the destiny of a nation: Yes we can.

It was whispered by slaves and abolitionists as they blazed a trail towards freedom through the darkest of nights: Yes we can.

It was sung by immigrants as they struck out from distant shores and pioneers who pushed westward against an unforgiving wilderness: Yes we can.

It was the call of workers who organized, **women who reached for the ballot…**Yes we can, to justice and equality…."[337]

This was probably the most powerful of all the speeches Barack Obama gave during the campaign. "Yes, we can!" became one of the most widely used slogans in the campaign. This speech was used as the script for the "Yes we can" video performed by will.i.am.[338] This video has been viewed over 26 million times on YouTube.[339]

Barack Obama told us that Yes, we can "reach for the ballot," reminding us of the struggle of women to gain the right to vote, and also the importance of exercising that right at this moment in history. We heard his words. We voted in record numbers. We determined the outcome of an election. Mothers, Grandmothers, and Professional Women from all over the country, who possess wisdom, who share my view of motherhood, who value character, who were desperate for change, turned out in record numbers to help elect Senator Barack Obama as our 44th President.

The majority of the people I met volunteering in Texas and Ohio, were young women, mothers and grandmothers. The person running the Dallas office was a woman. It was a woman who saw my yard sign, knocked on my door and invited me to an Obama rally of women at her home. The vast majority of people with whom I worked to register voters were women. It was mothers and grandmothers who sat outside the early voting polling place with me for seven days holding Obama signs and taking abuse from an occasional adversary. It was women shopping at the grocery store who would stop me and comment on my Obama shirt. It was a female attorney who stopped by our early-voting location to ensure that the person in-charge of the polling place was following the rules. It was a grandmother in Ohio, working next to me, who asked me to take her picture to prove to her unborn grandchild that she was a part of history. The woman I remember most vividly was a 66 year-old grandmother in Ohio who cried as she left the work-room on the last day of my service to the Ohio campaign. She spoke simply through quiet tears saying, "Thank you for coming to help. It means a lot to me." She knew what I am just discovering. She knew that together WE, the women who volunteered and turned out to vote, would make the difference not because of a woman's agenda, but because of our national agenda. We reached for the ballot and we made a difference! "Yes, We Did!"

It was Barack Obama's extraordinary character that made his message of hope resonate in all of us. We did not elect a man to the office of President of the United States who chose a beauty queen as his running mate. The first thing we heard about Sarah Palin, was that she was a former beauty queen.[340] Wait a minute! I don't watch those pageants any more. Why would I want someone to be the next Vice-President, and potentially the President of our country, whose main qualification is that she is beautiful; or at least some male judges in Alaska thought so a few years ago? Haven't we evolved? She doesn't believe in evolution,[341] but doesn't the rest of America? She doesn't blink but she winks during speeches! She is not the role model I want for my girls. I would like to respect the first female president, instead of laughing at her. Let's give a "shout out" to all the women of the country and say "Yes, we did!."

Chapter 7

Why Did Some Women Vote for McCain/Palin?

National results of the 2008 election

Forty three percent of women voting in the 2008 election cast their ballots for John McCain.[342] John McCain, who did not have a strong track record favoring "women's issues" strayed from his short list of potential VPs to choose a relatively unknown female.[343] For a very short time, some indicated that this pick was "brilliant and an unexpected pick."[344] While most would agree that the choice of Sarah Palin was "unexpected," it is now incontrovertible that this choice was far from "brilliant."

Obviously, the presence of a woman on the ticket in 2008 was not outcome-determinative.[345] Historically women don't vote for a candidate simply because a woman is on the ticket. Women tend to vote Democatic.[346] While many Clinton supporters hoped that Obama would select Clinton as his running mate, some Clinton supporters indicated an anti-Democratic feeling and formed PUMA(Party Unity My Ass).[347] PUMA was a group of men and women who had been Hillary supporters who were threatening to vote for McCain. While it's hard to believe that anyone who supported Hillary would vote for McCain, surely there were some. However Hillary's 18 million supporters obviously did not support McCain/Palin, or the result of the election of 2008 would have been dramatically different.[348] For most women abortion was a bigger issue, including those who were Republicans, Independents, and of course Democratic women.[349] Thus the issue of abortion alone produced a larger advantage for Democrats than the economy, the war, or health care.

Some women who thought Palin was sufficiently intelligent to handle the job, still questioned whether Palin could balance the demands of five children and the demands of the Presidency at the same time.[350] Even the male Presidents of the recent past didn't have to balance the competing needs of five children, including a special needs baby, and the demands inevitably placed upon the President. In fact five children in one family is quite unusual, even in Alaska. In 1987, US Census Bureau indicated that families were tending to have fewer children.[351] By 2000, the average number of children per family in the U.S. was .90.[352] In 2000 the state with the highest average number of children per family was Alaska at 1.14.[353] Thus when the majority of women in the U.S. wondered how Sarah Palin could balance 5 children and the job of Governor or Vice-President, we were not being "sexist" or "judgmental." We were being "realistic" or "practical." Fathers and mothers each feel challenged to meet the needs of five children …regardless of the parents' job(s) outside the home, and even if one parent stays home full-time.

The most amazing thing to me was that some educated women voted for McCain/Palin, knowing that Sarah Palin would be next in line to run this country. In my entire life I have never been so upset or disenchanted with politics, as when John McCain nominated Sarah Palin as his Vice-Presidential candidate. I was a Registered nurse, a trial attorney, and a stay-at-home mom for 15 years. I attended college for 7 years, making more A's than any other grade. I have raised three children, two of whom are college age, and attend one of the best schools in the country. Some people might call me a "soccer mom." However nothing about the experiences in my 52 years of life prepared me to serve as the Vice-President of this country. Never did I perceive that I was qualified, competent, or knowledgeable enough to be the President or Vice-President of this country. I am smart enough to appreciate what I do not know. I know Sarah Palin, the "hockey mom" was unfit to lead this country.

One woman's story

Every month I go to my neurologist for an IV infusion of a new medicine for the treatment of Multiple Sclerosis. Five chairs fill the small room where we receive the IV infusions, and all five chairs are always filled from 8:00 a.m. until after closing. The entire process takes an average of three hours, and during that time the patients in the other four chairs often share information about their lives, their disease, and the callers on their cell phones. Women are disproportionately affected by MS, so the majority of patients in this room are always women. Yet, the fact that we are women and each have M.S. is the only common bond we have. Our ages, races, religions, socio-economic status, and educational levels are diverse. Privacy is not a luxury we experience during these three hour visits.

During a recent visit, the male nurse was asking about the book I was writing. The patient sitting next to me inquired about my book. Having learned to be sensitive to the feelings and opinions of other patients, I am always careful to limit my obvious enthusiasm about Barack Obama, and my disdain for McCain/Palin. Being positioned for three hours next to someone who worked for the McCain/Palin team could be painful for all concerned if my true feelings were made known at the outset of the visit. The patient next to me was a woman of about 40 years of age, and mother of two boys, ages, 9 and 14. She said she voted for "Sarah Palin." At the time I found it interesting that she perceived her vote to be "for Sarah" instead of "for McCain," but I opted to say nothing. About twenty minutes later the same patient started speaking about personal problems in her marriage. She explained that she had recently determined that her husband was having an affair, and when she confronted him about the affair, he asked her "…so, what are you going to do about it?." The reality was that she couldn't do anything about it if she wanted to continue to receive medical care. This patient was blind in one eye, and only had limited vision in the other, due to her MS. She was not able to work outside the home, and couldn't drive because of her limited vision. Until being put on the IV medicine, she had been in a wheel chair, but now was able to walk, with great difficulty, with a cane. The obvious problem was that if she divorced her husband due to his infidelity, she would be left without medical insurance, and would certainly become completely blind, and perhaps return to a wheelchair. As I sat feeling totally distraught about this woman's burden, the battles fought by Barack Obama over health care reform seemed even more important. I wondered if she was aware of the effort Barack Obama had made to ensure health care for everyone. I wondered if she realized that if "Sarah Palin" had been elected, she would likely have no hope of escaping the intolerable attitude of her husband. She was a prisoner in her marriage.

Her vote for "Sarah Palin" was innocent. She thought Sarah was a "nice lady," and didn't know much else about the politics or social issues in the election of 2008. Maybe she didn't realize that the person who should earn our vote isn't necessarily the most attractive, or the one with whom we would like to go shopping. Women must be vigilant in our struggle to identify those politicians who are committed to Feminist objectives, and ensure that other women appreciate these attitudes. It is because of this patient, and women like her, that I am keenly aware of the importance of being an advocate for education for all people; especially women. "Empowering women" can't be limited to ensuring that an elite group of women are empowered to rise to become doctors, lawyers, and CEO's. When your focus is putting food on the table, a roof overhead, or health care for a loved one, involvement in politics seems a luxury many women can't afford. However we must all take an active role and do what we can toward protecting the health and well being of all women. It is the responsibility and the privilege of the women who have achieved professional success to do our part to facilitate the liberation of all women. There will never be a "convenient" time. We are all busy. One-fourth of women in America who receive health insurance through their husbands are especially at risk of losing coverage. Husbands may lose jobs and divorce remains high.[354] The time when a woman is most in need of governmental help is the moment when she has the least amount of time to devote to being active in politics.

It is our job to educate women, not to alienate them. If we are to facilitate change, it will only happen if the majority of the electorate perceives the importance of electing the particular candidate who is a true Feminist, not simply the one who calls herself a Feminist. It is not enough that the majority of women voted in 2008 for Barack Obama. We must seek to minimize the number of misinformed women in this country, who might support someone who appears to be different than she really is. We must protect against candidates who might say one thing, and do another.

Chapter 8

Strong Leaders

The women who were actively involved in the Obama campaign were amazing. According to the pundits, and those who touted themselves as being politically savvy, women were predominately supporting Hillary.[355] Each time I met another female supporter of Obama I would marvel at the fact that yet ANOTHER woman seemed to see what I did in Senator Obama. Soon it was clear to me that those reporting that women would favor Hillary weren't so politically savvy. *Many* women were supporting Senator Obama, even though he has a y chromosome, and he didn't wear lipstick. My personal assistant, our housekeeper, my best female friends, and women all around me were supporting Obama. I was NOT in the minority. The majority of women in Dallas County were supporting Barack Obama.[356] Women wanted the best candidate, regardless of his/her gender. As it turned out, the majority of women in the country wanted the best candidate, regardless of his/her gender, race, and/or religious affiliation.[357]

High profile women were vocal supporters during the primary. The Wisdom of these Women was apparent.

Michelle Obama

Michelle Obama is amazing. Having attended some of the best schools in the country, she graduated cum laude from Princeton University with a major in sociology and minor in African American studies.[359] After obtaining a Bachelor of Arts degree, she attended Harvard Law School.[360] With a JD from Harvard, she could have found a job in hundreds of firms nation-wide. She is bright, organized, responsible, articulate, insightful, and the master of multi-tasking. She is an example of a woman who could do anything professionally that she might choose. In spite of her professional abilities, Michelle has always made her children's interests, and those of her husband, a priority.[361] While the title of "First Lady" is impressive, it was probably not on the list of her professional goals, when she graduated from Harvard law school. Her sacrifices to facilitate the election of Barack Obama as the 44th President were sacrifices made for our benefit, and for which we should forever be grateful. Michelle Obama had the wisdom to recognize the importance of sharing her husband with the American people. Thank you Michelle!

Oprah

Oprah was one of the first celebrities to endorse Barack Obama.[362] Certainly the impact of an early, public endorsement by Oprah Winfrey was electrifying for the Obama campaign.[363] The first time I ever heard the name of Barack Obama was when Oprah endorsed him. My first thought was "…if Oprah thinks Barack Obama is worth supporting, I better find out who this guy is, because he is going to be our next President." I am not the only one who recognized how incredibly important it was that Oprah endorsed any candidate. One analysis estimates that her endorsement alone delivered over a million votes in the close 2008 Democrat Primary race.[364] According to some, Oprah is the most influential woman in the world.[365] Significantly, Oprah is the perfect example of a person who has overcome a century of discrimination. The press, and the public, no longer think of her as a Black woman, but simply as a woman. She is a media mogul, a philanthropist, an Emmy Award winner, and her show is the highest-rated talk show in the history of television.[366]

Oprah took a chance when she publically endorsed Obama.[367] It might have been said that she endorsed him just because he was African American. It might have been said that she was misusing her influence. Most of Oprah's viewers are women.[368] Especially because Hillary was still in the race, and perceived by some as the "woman's candidate," Oprah risked alienating a large number of her viewers.[369] Oprah didn't endorse Obama because of his gender, his race, his marital status, or the designer of his clothes. Oprah endorsed Obama because she knew he was our best hope for change in the country.

Oprah gave a very powerful speech at the L.A. rally. She explained that someone had accused her of being a "traitor." She explained why she was not a "traitor"…

> "I've been a woman all my life…
> I'm a free woman, and that means
> You get to think for yourself, and
> You get to decide for yourself what to do…
> So I am not a "traitor," and the truth has
> Lead me to Barack Obama…"[370]

Oprah had the wisdom to know that women, if we looked, would see what she saw in Obama. He is a leader. Oprah is a leader. Oprah demands respect, and Barack Obama is not afraid of a strong woman. He respects women. Thank you Oprah for having the wisdom to make sure that we paid attention! Thank you for having the wisdom to know that if we looked beyond gender we would find the best candidate.

Maria Shriver

Maria Shriver is the "First Lady" of California.[371] While Ms. Shriver is known by many because of her husband, the governor of California, Arnold Schwarzenegger,[372] her role as a leader of strong women is apparent. Maria is an award winning journalist, a best-selling author, and a mother. She sponsors the Women's Conference every year, with the goal of inspiring women to make change happen in their personal lives and their communities.[373] In early February of 2008, before the primary in California, Maria appeared with Michelle Obama, and Oprah at a Women's Rally in Los Angeles, to endorse Obama.[374] Her endorsement was important for many reasons. She was openly endorsing the candidate who was running against a woman, and who was not the candidate endorsed by her husband, the

Governor of California. Her public endorsement of Obama, gave women across the country a role model. She was a very public example to all women- that it was O.K. to support a candidate other than the one supported by your husband. Her reasons for supporting Obama were articulated in a way that was well thought out, clear, and easily understood.[375]

"...If he were a state he would be California....

Diverse, independent, open, smart, innovative, inspiring, dreamer, bucks tradition, leader..."

"But this is a moment. It's a moment to have a conversation with yourself. Do I believe in an America that's about unity, about coming together, it's about seeing beyond the labels? We've got to see beyond the labels that divide us. And if that's the kind of America I want, I think it will be very clear to you what you should do on Tuesday."[376]

She was not only showing her support for Obama, but also demonstrating to women that bright, liberated women might choose to support the candidate who was not female. She was demonstrating to all women the importance of choosing a candidate based upon factors other than his/her gender. Women do not want to be treated differently based upon their gender, so Maria was reminding us not to choose our candidate for President based upon gender. Thank you Maria for having the wisdom to make your own decisions, regardless of the political position of your husband!

Caroline Kennedy

Caroline Kennedy also appeared at the LA rally supporting Senator Obama.[377] Women identify with Caroline because of her strong character and intellect. As a writer, and lawyer, and a mother, we can admire her for her contribution to the campaign.[378] At the rally Caroline made a personal connection between her father, John F. Kennedy, and Barack Obama.[379] It was Caroline's observation that people reacted to Barack Obama much in the same way they had to her father. She reminded us of the charismatic character of her father, and compared Barack Obama to him.[380] Again, she was not supporting Hillary in the primary. Obama was her choice. Again, she was a reminder that women should choose their candidate on the basis of the character and leadership, instead of gender. It was also significant that Caroline was a resident of New York, Hillary's home state. Thank you Caroline for having the wisdom to identify the candidate that was most like your father!

Maria Elena Durazo

Maria Elena Durazo endorsed Barack Obama at the LA Rally with Michelle, Oprah, Maria, and Caroline. While not a celebrity, the effect of Ms. Durazo's endorsement of Obama, and her commitment to the campaign equaled or exceeded the importance of these celebrities. Ms. Durazo is the current Executive Secretary-Treasurer of the Los Angeles County Federation of Labor, AFL-CIO. In this capacity, Ms. Durazo heads an organization of more than 800,000 union members which is the biggest regional labor group in California.[381] She is the past president of the UNITE-HERE local 11.[382] Not only did she take a leave from her job to campaign for Obama, but she served as the national co-chair of the Obama for President Campaign committee, and was a pledged delegate at the National Convention. Maria is an example of a leader of men and women, who happens to be a woman. She is also an example of a professional woman who gave of her time to work for the campaign. Thank you Maria for having the wisdom to dedicate yourself to the election of Barack Obama!

Susan Eisenhower

Susan Eisenhower is the grand-daughter of Dwight Eisenhower.[383] Ms. Eisenhower endorsed Obama in the Washington Post article published Feb. 2, 2008, just one day before the rally in Los Angeles. Susan Eisenhower eloquently described why she was supporting Obama:

> "...I am not alone in worrying that my generation will fail to do what my grandfather's did so well: Leave America a better, stronger place than the one it found....
>
> It is in this great tradition of crossover voters that I support Barack Obama's candidacy for President. If the Democratic Party chooses Obama as its candidate, this life-long Republican will work to get him elected and encourage him to seek strategic solutions to meet America's greatest challenges. To be successful, our President will need bipartisan help."[384]

By her public endorsement, Susan showed the American people, and especially women, that if Obama were the Democratic choice, some Republicans would support him. Without saying it directly, she was demonstrating by her enthusiasm for Obama that she, and many other Republicans, might support Obama. She was clear that Hillary would not be a person who could unite the country. The effect of her endorsement was to demonstrate in a tangible way, that Obama had bi-partisan support of women. Thank you Susan for your wisdom in selecting your candidate based upon values, character, and education. Thank you for having the wisdom to demand that any candidate who would win your vote would first demand that women be treated with respect!

Gloria Steinem

Ms. Steinem, an American feminist icon, is a writer, journalist, social and political activist, and has been identified by some as the "feminist godmother."[385] Born in 1934, Ms. Steinem, gained national prominence, and by 1969 was the founder of the *New York* magazine. Later she founded *Ms. Magazine*. In 1969 I was 12 years old. At that time I was not acquainted with any of the organizations Ms. Steinem had founded. Most of the women in Oklahoma in 1969 understood that for which Ms. Steinem was fighting, but they were unwilling to become soldiers in her army. During her career Ms. Steinem has published multiple books,[386] and founded many organizations, including the National Women's Political Caucus, the Women's Action Alliance, the Coalition of Labor Union Women, the Women Media Center, Choice USA, NOW, the coalition of Labor Union Women, Voters for Choice, the Foundation for Women, and feminist.com.[387] Ms. Steinem convened the historic 1971 Women's Political Caucus.[388]

A "Women Against Sarah Palin" web site was initiated after the nomination of Sarah Palin as John McCain's running mate. An article by Gloria Steinem is featured on this site. Ms. Steinem explained…

"Palin shares nothing but a chromosome with Clinton"[389]

"Palin's value to those patriarchs is clear: She opposes just about every issue that women support by a majority or plurality…"[390]

While Ms. Steinem initially supported Hillary, she became an outspoken supporter for Barack Obama in the general election.[391] By becoming an advocate for Obama, after previously backing Hillary, Ms. Steinem set an example for women around the country that women, who previously supported a female candidate, should not favor the McCain/Palin ticket, just because Sarah Palin had chromosomes similar to Hillary's. Thank you Gloria for having the wisdom to help women in America elect the candidate who demands respect for all women!

Women were the difference. Women exercised our right to vote and our freedom of speech as we have not done in the history of our country. Success didn't happen by accident, but it resulted from the commitment of thousands of women nationally. From celebrities like Oprah, to the stay-at-home moms, whose names might be unknown, it was the individual effort of so many, doing what each of us could, that made the difference. It is with gratitude that I reflect upon the roles that each of these women played in this historic election. It is also with gratitude that I reflect upon the people who did not live long enough to realize the dream of equality. In spite of, or perhaps because of, the nomination of Sarah Palin, women raised our voices and we were heard. Sarah Palin does not represent the majority of women in this country. Anyone who continues to believe that she is OUR leader must believe everything Sarah says.

Chapter 9

The Defining Moment

Barack Obama, one of the great orators of the 21st century, gave his acceptance speech in Chicago on Nov. 4, 2008. He explained to the crowd of over 100,000 people,... "This is the defining moment in history..."[392] President-Elect Obama was referring to the moment when history was written for the entire country. He made reference to Whites, Blacks, Latinos, Asians, American Indians, Republicans, Democrats, Young, Old, Disabled and those who are not disabled, and all who turned out to support him.[393] Barack Obama explained that for the first time in history, all these groups came together, for the common purpose of change. "Change has come to America" he proclaimed.[394] It was also the **Defining Moment for Women**! In our wisdom, women chose our 44th President. The majority of voters in the election of 2008 included Whites, Blacks, Latinos, Asians, American Indians, Republicans, Democrats, Young, Old, Disabled and those not disabled,... but the **majority** of those voters were...WOMEN.

Empires have been "defined" by wars, won or lost. Countries are characterized by significant moments in their history. When the first man walked on the moon, people around the world were watching. On 9-11 when the World Trade Center was destroyed, with hundreds of lives permanently erased, the world took note. When Barack Obama was elected as our 44th President, the entire world celebrated. People around the world recognized that the election of 2008 was a defining moment in the history of the United States, and perhaps the entire world. The election had global significance because of the skin color of the new President, because of his character and values, and because WOMEN were responsible for the majority of votes for him.

For over a century, women have been at "war." We had been fighting for our freedom from oppression. We were fighting for equal rights. We were fighting for fundamental fairness. Our weapons were not guns or swords. Our weapon in this fight for our freedom and equal rights was wisdom. We did not resort to violence. We fought with our spirits, our words, and our dedication to a cause which was greater than all of us! In our wisdom we knew that victory would not be limited to women, but it would be a triumph for mankind. It was not a handful of celebrities making a difference, although they were part of the many that did their part. It was millions of women working, campaigning, and voting. The election of 2008 was a Defining Moment in our history because of the commitment of Millions of Women. It was a time that women of the United States of America came together purely and simply for the benefit of mankind.[395] Because women in the United States are liberated, and had the wisdom to reach for the ballot, women around the world have the benefit of new leadership.

It seems such a fundamental principle of humanity, that every life is sacred. Yet it wasn't until now that women worked together to ensure the sanctity of life for all of humanity. Soldiers have fought for "freedom" throughout the history of our country. Women have been the soldiers within our country fighting for "freedom" from a different kind of oppression. We have won our "freedom"! Now that we have tasted the sweetness of that freedom, we will savor it, and we will always expect that same sweetness every day of our lives. It may take another generation to ensure the freedom from oppression for women around the world, but at least the fight has begun, and we have a stronger, more united, leadership team.

The election is over but the involvement of women around the country is just beginning. From the White House, to meetings in our living rooms, women are engaged. We are committed to making a difference. The problems facing the country are still overwhelming, but the difference is that women are now taking an active role in finding solutions. We have the wisdom to be patient, looking for permanent solutions, instead of "quick fixes." We represent the combined strength of (1) the next generation through the children we have raised, (2) the strength of businesswomen, celebrities, and politicians, and (3) women who are willing to volunteer their time, their minds and hearts, to make the world a better place. Sarah Palin is not a member of any of these segments of the population. The chorus has been heard, and we now know the lyrics. It may ultimately take many repetitions of our song, but we will not tire. We know the words by heart, and we remain resolute. The sound of our voices rings in the largest cities and the smallest villages around the world. It may be translated into many languages, and may be heard on a multitude of stages. The volume increases with each passing day. We can only hope that one day Sarah Palin will hear our song, and become part of the chorus. Until that day we will remain vigilant. Women must continue to speak out against any person who might slow our evolution or limit our progress.

Wisdom

Webster defines "wisdom" as:

"the quality of being wise; power of judging rightly and following the soundest course of action, based upon knowledge, experience, understanding, etc.; good judgment; sagacity ... learning; knowledge; erudition...a wise plan or course of action."[396] Women in our wisdom elected the candidate in 2008 who embodied the values, character, intellect, and leadership ability that our country needed. We disregarded gender. We have proved through our votes that we are not hypocrites. For greater than a century we have objected to consideration of gender. Our votes in November of 2008 demonstrate that we disregard gender. We voted for the male candidate, even though a woman was on the ticket. We voted based upon our perception of the best opportunity for change in the country, instead of favoring the candidate with reproductive organs similar to our own.

Sarah Palin was an embarrassment to women. Her education was limited, her experience was lacking, and her judgment was flawed. Sarah lacked basic knowledge that was exploited in every facet of the media. She was unimpressive as a professional woman, and as a mother. She was not the person women would choose to represent us as the first female Vice-President of our country.

Survival of the Fittest

Charles Darwin would describe the "change" that came to America in November of 2008 as "natural selection" or the theory of "survival of the fittest." We evolved, not because of some noble, ambitious effort to rectify years of oppression, but because we were fighting for survival as a nation. Survival required that we elect the *fittest* and most capable candidate, re-gardless of race or gender. The evolutionary path of women and Blacks in America has been perilous. The soldiers on that path have endured torture and some have paid with their lives. With each generation since Thomas Jefferson, we have evolved. With the birth of each generation, we made progress. Through the process of "natural selection" a leader emerged who would fight for our survival. In this case, the species didn't select him be-cause he was the prettiest (although he might be the most color-ful), or because he was a member of the dominant sex. Our selection was based upon his ability to lead, and our perception that he was the best suited to ensure our survival. As the moth-ers of the next generation, we fought for survival, and we won!

Without minimizing the significance of an African-American being elected to the highest office in the land, turning out voters in record numbers, unifying people regardless of their age, race, religion, and even party affiliation, we must not fail to recognize the significance, and the impact, of women in this election. For over 100 years women have been fighting for equal rights. Until the election of 2008, it seemed that it was a minority of women who were active in this fight, and who personalized the passion for a society in which women would be treated equally with men. The involvement and votes of women were particularly impressive because of the involvement of Sarah Palin.

For too long, too many women have been willing to be treated as second class citizens. Just because women had the right to vote, did not mean that any individual woman would in fact exercise that right. If she did, would there be sufficient num-bers of women to follow in her footsteps to ensure success at the end of the day? Until now, many women, myself included, did not take advantage of the opportunity to have an impact. Some simply voted as they were instructed by their husbands. Others were just unwilling to take time out of their day to cast their single vote, which they perceived would not make a difference. Never Again! Perhaps we should thank Sarah Palin, because she motivated women to vote...against her.

The United States census reports indicate that as of October 1, 2007, women in America out numbered men by 3.6 million.[397] Women are more educated than our male counter-parts.[398] Seven percent more women than men, ages 25-29 had attained a bachelor's degree or higher in 2006.[399] The Bureau also projected that in 2007-2008 women would earn 59% of the bachelor's degrees and 61% of the master's degrees awarded.[400] Not surprisingly, women are projected to earn a majority (52%) of first-professional degrees, such as law and medicine.[401] This appears to be a trend, indicating women are gaining ground as educated leaders in our society. Since 1991 the proportion of young women enrolled in college has exceeded the enrollment rate for men, and the gap has widened over time.[402] The implication of these statistics is staggering, especially because the life expectancy of women exceeds that of men by approximately 5 years.[403] The clear message is that women currently constitute the majority of the electorate. This majority is predicted to increase, and at the same time women are increasingly becoming the more educated portion of the population. The number of women-owned businesses grew 20% between 1997 and 2002, which was twice the national average.[404] This growth is indicative of a trend. By 2008, there were approximately 10.1 million privately-held businesses in which women owned 50% or more of the company.[405] These companies generate an estimated $1.9 trillion dollars in annual sales and employ 13 million people nationwide.[406] It is estimated that 2 in 5 businesses in the U.S. are now owned by women, representing 40% of all businesses in the country.[407] Given the fact that women are out-living men, and gaining more education than men, we could expect these numbers to increase. One source estimates that $41 trillion dollars will pass from one generation to the next over the next 50 years, and it will pass to women.[408] Because women are responsible for 83% of all consumer purchases,[409] women are going to have the money, and we will determine how it is spent. Politicians who do not respect women and listen to our concerns will pay the price. Women are educated, knowledgeable, and we are becoming leaders in business. We have found our voices and they will be heard in all future elections. Minimizing the importance of women will surely be the downfall of any candidate.

Even in the election of 2004, 65% of female citizens reported voting, while only 62% of men reported voting.[410] We must also note the importance of the time women volunteer. Women volunteer much more often than men do, for all causes. The U.S. Census Bureau in the Women's History Month, March of 2008, reported that 30% of women volunteer, as compared to only 23% of men.[411] Overall, 36 million women perform unpaid volunteer activities.[412] Thus, the number of women volunteering for the Barack Obama campaign was not an accident, or an aberration. Women are willing to work hard to accomplish our goals, even in the absence of financial remuneration. Yes We Did!

Given the importance of the support and vote of women, we need to understand why women favored Barack Obama. It wasn't his gender. To some it may have been his race, but the majority of women who supported him were of a different race than he.[413] Perhaps there was a character trait in Barack Obama that we recognized as being different from most politicians, and was a trait we would like to see in our "public servants." As mothers we learn to give of ourselves, sacrificing things that we might do for ourselves, for the sake of a child. Barack Obama tells the story of his Grandmother who made the choice to forgo a new dress for herself to make sure he had what he needed.[414] That selflessness is a trait that can best be learned by example, and Barack Obama had that example in his life. Now he gives back to others every day of his life. In speeches he is heard to wish for a better country for his girls. He verbalizes his desire to ensure that his children have the same opportunity that he did growing up. As a "community organizer" he demonstrated his willingness to sacrifice what could have been a very lucrative life as an attorney in a big firm to help the people of Chicago. This character trait, of being charitable and selfless, is rare in politicians today.

Women identify with this trait. If Barack Obama's politics were not enough to make women identify with him, his charitable spirit and selfless attitude resonated in all of us. It is gratifying to realize that as women have become more liberated, we have not lost our commitment to serving others. By ensuring the election of Barack Obama, we have helped to serve others in our country at a time when we needed change more than any other time in recent history. To all the women involved in the campaign, thank you. To all the women who stood in line to vote, thank you. To all the women who have taught their children the importance of doing for others, thank you. To all the women who looked past the gender, race, religion, sexual preferences of the candidates, and selected their candidate based upon his/her character, value, attitudes, and leadership abilities, I thank you.

THIS WAS A DEFINING MOMENT IN HISTORY FOR WOMEN. Because of the sheer number of women who voted, because of the sizeable financial contributions of women, because of the thousands of hours women volunteered in this election, because of the thousands of people influenced by women, and because the majority of the votes cast for Barack Obama were votes of women, this American victory was also a victory for women. It was the wisdom of millions of women that turned the possibility of change into a reality. Throughout the history of the United States, women have never had such an impact upon any election. Never again will a man underestimate the power of our voices, without being proved to be wrong. Women recognized just how important this election was for the future of our country. Women chose a candidate, without regard to gender. In spite of the fact that there were female candidates, who could have attracted the women's vote, women relied upon their years of acquired wisdom, and voted based upon their values, instead of merely considering gender. Three conclusions are incontrovertible. The first is that the percentage of women voting in presidential races has increased in the last three elections; 2000-61%, 2004 65%, and 2008 66%.[415] The second is that there are approximately 5 million more women than men in the U.S.[416] and the number of women is increasing.[417] The third is that the life expectancy of women is roughly 5-6 years longer than men.[418] Thus, the number of women in the U.S. is increasing, the percentage of women voting is increasing, and therefore the number of women voting is increasing.[419] We have realized the power of our voices; we constitute the majority of the electorate;[420] and over time that majority will grow larger. In the election of 2008 women stood up and shouted "Yes, we can!"

Let us never forget the importance of standing up for the principles that make this country strong. Women around the world are still treated like chattels. We can be their role models helping them stand up to the men who would enslave them. Let us each appreciate the battles fought before us, and those ahead of us yet to be fought. If we are to be "good mothers" to our children, and if we are to be good Americans, we must always take an active role in determining elections. We must always "reach for the ballot." We DID in this election, and forever more we will stand up and make a difference! It will be our continuing responsibility to educate ourselves about candidates, and ensure that those around us, especially other women, are also informed.

Today, I stand up and shout, "**Yes, We Did**!" We used our education, intellect, and wisdom to get past gender, and race, and voted for the best candidate. Women in America had the wisdom to fight for a better future for ourselves and our children. We stood up against a woman who was not qualified and who did not have the intellect to run the country. "**Yes We Did**!" We voted in record numbers and we comprised the majority of voters. Barack Obama was right when he said: "Yes, we can." We can, and **We DID**"!

Inauguration Day 2009[421]

The Journey Traveled

"Coming of age" is a term used to describe the transition from adolescence to adulthood. This transition may occur at different times in different cultures. Within the same culture, the transition may occur at different ages depending upon each person's particular circumstances. I thought I was an adult by the time I was 20 years old. However my "coming of age" in fact, took almost half a century. It took Women as a group almost an entire century to make our transition to "adulthood." The election of 2008 embodied the very essence of that transition. The personalities in the election of 2008 characterize the journey traveled. John McCain represents men from an extinct era, in which society tolerated the treatment of women as "trim." Sarah Palin represents women who are willing to tolerate being treated as "trim."

Barack Obama is a man, abandoned by his father, and raised by women. He respects all people based upon their character and values, instead of the color of their skin, their gender, or their sexual preferences. Michelle Obama is a professional woman who sacrificed her career, to be a stay-at-home-mom, for the sake of her children, her husband, and our country. We don't think of Michelle as "just a mom." We don't think less of her because she "opted out" of her professional life as an attorney. It is a cast of characters who graphically illustrate the journey traveled and our arrival at our destination. The wisdom of women is that we accurately perceived each of the characters in the election of 2008, and voted accordingly. We have made the difficult transition to adulthood. We rejected a man who treats women as "trim." Our vote for Barack Obama for President, and our vote for Michelle Obama for the position of First Lady, was a way that the women of the United States showed that we demand that women earn and be treated with respect and honor. We were voting for a strong leadership team. The election of 2008 had everything to do with race, gender, and Wisdom.

We are strong because we care. We were victorious because we were committed. We are united because of our common purpose. We will continue to make a difference, because our eyes have been opened, and they will not close. We have been awakened from our slumber, and we will not tire. As care-givers we have shown the ultimate benevolence, by working to facilitate change not just for our own benefit, but for the entire country, and for the entire world. Nothing can stand in the way of the power of women calling for change. The future is in our hands. Let us shape the future of our country with the same dedication and commitment that we have demonstrated in raising our children. If we are to raise happy, successful children, then we must ensure that the country in which they live is filled with hope and possibility. If we dedicate our time, energy, enthusiasm, and love, the result will be a country in which all children will achieve their potential. We have become the care-givers of our country. It is not enough to raise good kids, if the country in which they live is failing to thrive. We have an obligation to all children, to make their world a better place, and their future brighter. We have become the protectors of our country. Having accepted this challenge, we must always dedicate ourselves to nurturing our country with the same commitment and love that we have for our children.

We must give our daughters a road map of the journey traveled. We must show them the way. Our daughters must embark upon this journey with us, knowing that the journey will never end. If they choose a partner or spouse, it must be a person who will be willing to travel with them, and support them along the way. We must teach all children, boys and girls, how to pack for the journey. They must not fill their suitcases with unnecessary clutter. Personal values and character are the most essential travel companions. There should be appreciation and respect for fellow travelers. Some may take longer to reach their destination, so we must be patient. The travelers must demonstrate compassion for those who fall along the way. We can help them to walk again. Some may deviate from the path. We can help them find their way. Educate others by showing them the path. We can never reach our destination if we travel the path alone. Future generations must appreciate the path behind, and the path ahead. Pack this book in your suitcase as a reminder of the path behind. You know the path ahead. Don't worry about traveling at night as you, yourself, are a light that will illuminate the path ahead. Never let your light dim. We will be the guiding light for all travelers who embark upon this journey.

Sarah Palin never obtained a passport to enable her to embark upon this journey. If she would consider leaving some of her unnecessary baggage behind, and if she indicated a willingness to obtain a passport, many women could show her the way.

Chapter 10

Time to Retire Sarah

Laughing Out Loud

Sarah Palin is no longer the potential Vice-President of our country, she is not the Governor of Alaska, and it appears she is not even the actual author of her book (Lynn Vincent wrote it). Because she is not currently a threat to our way of life, I can now laugh out loud at the many jokes made over the last year about Sarah Palin. There is something therapeutic and satisfying about laughing at something that could have been so dangerous, and is now no longer a threat. We can laugh out loud…together.

The most amazing and vivid demonstration of Sarah Palin's lack of insight or perception of the world around her was Palin's interview, given while turkeys were being be-headed in the background. Even after the reporters gave her the option to do the interview in another location, Sarah indicated that the location was perfectly appropriate, and voluntarily participated in the interview, explaining that:

1. "This was neat" she said of the outing.

2. "…you need a little bit of levity in this job…"

3. "…it's nice to do something to promote a local business…"

4. it's nice to "…just participate in something that isn't so heavy-handed politics that invites criticism."

5. "Certainly, we'll probably invite criticism for even doing this, too, but at least this was fun."[422]

A Canadian talk show took advantage of poor Sarah in their show, suggesting that she was talking to French President Sarkozy.[423] In that conversation Palin was told that the President could see Belgium from his house, and he referenced his love for "killing those animals."[424] In over five minutes of conversation Palin seemed to be oblivious to the outrageous comments of a comedian.[425]

Internet jokes have been abundant. In fact the search words "Palin Jokes" results in 205,000 web sites that feature Palin Jokes.[426]While it is clear that Sarah never said the things these comedians were talking about, the jokes did make us think about things Sarah really said or did. Consider these jokes:

- I know all about Iran. I ran for Mayor and then I ran for Governor!

- I can't comment on the Kyoto Accord as I've only ever seen the Honda.

- My pregnant daughter is definitely going to marry the baby's father, John Edwards… I mean Levi Johnston

- I look forward to negotiating with the Shi'ites, as I haven't had a good one all week.

- I wouldn't want to go over to Kabul. I'm perfectly happy with my Direct T.V.

- I think that the drop in the price of stock is a good thing, as now people will be able to make their soups cheaper.

- I know how to deal with Hamas. With a side of eggs.

- I told John McCain I don't know how to deal with the nasty rumors about me on the internet! John replied "what's the internet?"

- I know all about Russia. I tried to get my brother-in-law to play their Roulette.

- When I started with Yahoo Mail I thought it was a guy who liked to party!

- I don't know about Fidel Castro, but Todd has a Gibson Guitar.

- I'm sure victory in Iraq is in the Bag, Dad.

- I'd deal with a Prime Minister Tzipi in the same way I'd deal with Dee, Doo and Dah.

- When I'm Vice President I won't discuss government top-secrets on Yahoo Mail. Hotmail is much more secure.

- I'm sorry that the Lehman Brothers went bankrupt as I really loved their bagels.

- I'm highly qualified as a diplomat: I have a high school diplomat.

- I'm against free trade. I think other countries should pay for our products.

- I welcome Israeli involvement in the West Bank if they can keep it from failing.

- I support government bailouts. After all, as Governor I bailed out of that damn bridge.

- I'm sure that was Barack Obama on TV winning the U.S. Open before his knee gave out.

- I oppose the Lisbon Treaty. I believe women should marry men.

- Does The Bush Doctrine mean he has a female physician?

- I am well equipped for international diplomacy as I speak in many tongues.

- I'm not worried about winning re-election in 2012 as the Apocalypse will have hit by then.

- I thought it was terrible that the Bank of America Lynched Merrill!

- I'm well equipped to be John McCain's Vice President. I took the Alaska Red Cross CPR class.

- Palestinians? Is that what my supporters are calling themselves?

- The CNN reporter asked me about Ahmadinejad, so I said Gesundheit.

- I know how to deal with Putin. I got the last one who did that to marry my daughter.

- No, the sign should say McCain-Palin 2008, not Geezer-Gidget 2008!

- I'm so happy that John asked me to accompany him to Vienna, Ohio. That makes three international capitals that I've visited!

- I believe illegal aliens should be deported and their flying saucers impounded.

- I'm glad the Italian government has shut down their local Al Qaeda group: Alitalia.

- I don't think the U.S. should get involved in Kashmir. I prefer Mohair.

- Of course I'm ready to be President! It's not like Bush is a hard act to follow.

- John McCain is correct in stating that the US economy is strong, but smell isn't everything. [427]

Rachel Maddow:

See her discussion of Sarah's "Pie Spy" business?[428]

Jimmy Fallon:

"Sarah Palin's 400-page memoir is going to be released on November 17th, and it's called *Going Rogue: An American Life*. And critics say that it starts out okay, it get's really exciting and then confusing, and then the last 100 pages are blank."

Jon Stewart

"As I watched the press conference, I realized finally we have a candidate for the people who loved George Bush's certainty but was bothered by his rationality and executive experience."

Jay Leno

"Sarah Palin is all over the news lately. She told Matt Lauer on the 'Today' show that, yes, the rumors were true, on election night she did want to deliver her own concession speech and she was disappointed that she couldn't. Well, she shouldn't feel bad. Wait till 2012. Deliver it then."

"Well, according to a new post-election survey, people want Sarah Palin to run for president in 2012. It says she's been getting thousands of calls from people pleading with her to run, all Democrats."

David Letterman:

"People in Alaska are looking forward to Sarah Palin's memoir. They're already calling it 'The Book to Nowhere.'"

"Friends of Governor Palin are saying that she is resigning because she is tired of attacks from the media. Thank God I didn't say anything."

"Now how about this, ladies and gentlemen? The Governor of Alaska, Sarah Palin, has announced she is stepping down. She will no longer be the Governor of Alaska. First thing, she woke up and went out on her porch and waved goodbye to Russia."

"And people are puzzled by this. They say, 'Well Governor, Sarah, what are you going to do? What's going to happen?' And insiders believe that she hopes to be the next 'Octomom.' But I don't know."

"A lot of public figures do this. When you have trouble, you blame the media. And today as a matter of fact she was up in a helicopter shooting Wolf Blitzer."

"I'll tell you, to be honest, I was quite nervous about this whole thing. And I was really nervous about an apology to Sarah Palin. So what I did to get my confidence up, to get my nerves to settle down, I rehearsed by apologizing to Tina Fey."[429]

Conan O'Brien

"According to a new poll, 42% of Americans say they would vote for Sarah Palin for president in 2012. They also said they'd support her decision to step down in 2013."

"Since resigning as governor, many say Sarah Palin is now going to spend some time working on her memoirs. Alaskans are saying they can't wait to start reading Palin's memoirs and then quit halfway through."

"In a recent study, the United States was ranked the 114th happiest country in the world. Then Sarah Palin stepped down. Now we're at 17."

"It's an emotional day. A lot of us are still mourning the loss of one of America's most entertaining figures, who left us all too soon. But don't worry, folks, Sarah Palin will be back. Comedians everywhere are praying."

"President Obama right now is in Russia. Obama went there because from Russia you can actually see Sarah Palin cleaning out her office in Alaska."

"This is true, according to a new report, I was reading this today in the paper, thousands of pregnant mothers in this country are planning to name their baby Barack. That's true. Yeah, after hearing this, Sarah Palin told Bristol, 'Don't even think about it.'"

David Letterman's:

Things More Fun than Reading Sarah Palin's Memoirs:

61 Getting run over by a lawnmower.

#14 Driving into a tree.

#45 Walking into traffic.

(no number) drinking my own pee.[430]

David Letterman's:

Top Ten Surprises in the Sarah Palin Memoir:

#10 She's already completed her 2012 Presidential concession speech.

#9 Her husband Todd is a person of interest in dozens of unsolved snowmobile hit and runs.

#8 State Troopers have been instructed to taser Katie Couric on site.

#7 "Memoir" is misspelled.

#6 Not only can she see Russia, earlier today she saw the astronauts working on the Hubble.

#5 The entire thing was plagiarized, word for word, from Artie Lange's *Too Fat to Fish*.

#4 The cover shows her in a passionate embrace with a shirtless Fabio.

#3 Sarah's sworn in as Governor with her left hand on *Guns and Amo* magazine.

#2 She had three-way sex with Michael Phelps and a stripper.

#1 Sarah Palin voted for Obama.[431]

The Same but Different

Barack Obama gave this country a gift long before he was elected president. By becoming a candidate for President he gave each of us a reason to be hopeful. Barack Obama was awarded the Nobel Peace prize in his first year in office because he inspired hope throughout the world.[432] "Only very rarely has a person to the same extent as Obama captured the world's attention and given its people hope for a better future. His diplomacy is founded in the concept that those who are to lead the world must do so on the basis of values and attitudes that are shared by the majority of the world's population."[433] Before the outcome of the election was known, we were already hopeful. Through his example, millions of people of all races around the world supported him as a candidate. We joined together in making a statement to the entire world, that racism in the United States would no longer be tolerated. We didn't elect Barack Obama because he was Black but because we have evolved. With this election the majority of Americans have shown by their vote that the years of hatred, bigotry, and racism have come to an end. There may still be a small segment of the population that wrongfully believes in the supremacy of white, male, heterosexuals, but as of November 4, 2008 they are a minority in America. With time this portion of the population will become extinct, and our grandchildren will only know them by what they read in their history books.

This is the next chapter in my attempt to make a difference. Observations and attitudes towards women and people of different races, need to be reduced to writing, to ensure that people in the future understand that change came in 2008, and why. Women, after this election, will never be the same. There is real hope that men in America have learned that women object to being treated as "TRIM." Any man who doesn't respect women will reap the whirlwind. Barack Obama has helped women realize that their involvement in the political process can have a determinative effect on the outcome of an election, and upon our entire culture. Our politics may be diverse, but our demand for respect is universal. Whatever issues may be close to the heart of any particular female voter, the majority of women have one issue that is a core value. As a starting point, women demand to be treated as equals. We demand that women who are our leaders insist upon respect as well. Women can speak proudly of motherhood without conveying a lack of education, political savvy, or knowledge of world affairs. Women can, and should, speak out emphatically about their unwillingness to tolerate abuse. The vote of women in this election is evidence of our resoluteness. No longer do we need to raise our voices to be heard. Our votes in this election *showed* the world that women will persevere. "Nothing can stand in the way of the power of millions of voices calling for change...Yes, we can...,"[434] and "Yes, We Did!"

John McCain will probably always perceive women as 'trim," but he will make sure the next Republican candidate for President is NOT a beauty queen. Dick Cheney is still hunting, but friends who hunt with him have learned to stay behind him. Sarah may still be shooting wolves from helicopters, hunting moose, and doing harm to the home of the Polar Bear, but maybe she will get a stamp or two in her passport; maybe when she waves to Russia they won't have to wave back because they don't care who she is; maybe she will subscribe to a newspaper; maybe she will run out of ammunition for her guns; and maybe this book will not be banned from the Wasilla library. Sarah will still celebrate Thanksgiving by visiting the turkey farm, but maybe this year nobody will be interviewing her while she does. I wonder who will attend the Thanksgiving feast at Sarah's house in 2009. Will some of the relatives be able to make parole in time for dinner? The Republican Party still has Sarah Palin's expensive clothes in garbage bags, but maybe they will be donated to the Smithsonian, to remember an era gone bye.

Now when I watch Sarah on television, I can laugh because she is not the next potential Vice-President of our country. She is not the Governor of Alaska. She is not even the Mayor of Wasilla. Women have demonstrated by our votes that she is not our leader. She may have gained financial security for her family but she is not compromising the security of our nation. Perhaps women around the country who voted for John McCain and Sarah Palin in 2008 are better informed, and perhaps they will not make the same mistake again. Sometimes we learn best by our mistakes, and maybe the Republican party has learned something from the Rogue.

Epilogue

Having experienced the joy of children in my life, I hope that all women can experience that same joy. Unfortunately not all children are born healthy, some women can't conceive or give birth, and some children may not be perceived as a "blessing" due to the financial challenges of raising a child. The birth of a child to a teenage girl may represent a direct interference with that teenager's ability to complete her education, pursue a career, mature as a woman, achieve her life goals, and establish her independence from parents or men. Relationships with men are challenging, and the addition of children may enhance or hinder that relationship. Children inevitably represent a permanent change in a woman's life. The age of the girl or woman at the birth of the first child may have a determinative effect upon the life of the child and the mother. One-third of the girls in the United States became pregnant before age 20, and more than 432,000 babies were born to women ages 15-19 in 2006. Women and girls will continue to have children. The only question is the age of the girl/woman when she begins having children. If women are to be truly liberated, we must do what we can to ensure that women have children when they are physically, emotionally, and financially ready to do so. Having children before achieving success in any of these areas can present a significant risk to the woman and her offspring. Education alone may be the single most important factor to achieving emotional and financial independence of a woman and her offspring. It would be a rare teenage girl who could manage a pregnancy, a child, and the completion of her education. A teenage pregnancy often results in dependence of the teenage girl on her parents, or on a man, for the entirety of her adult life. The implications for the child of a teenage mother are equally dramatic. The impact of becoming a teenage parent on the father in our society does not carry the same long term, and potentially devastating effects, as those felt by the mother.

Planned Parenthood Federation of America is a trusted health care provider, an informed educator, a passionate advocate, and a global partner helping similar organizations around the world. Planned Parenthood delivers vital reproductive health care, sex education, and information to millions of women, men, and young people worldwide.

In an effort to make a difference, a portion of any profit from the sale of this book will be donated to Planned Parenthood in honor of Sarah Palin. By purchasing this book, you and I together are attempting to make a difference. Thank you!

KEEPING IN TOUCH

If you are interested in monitoring our progress in raising money for Planned Parenthood, or would like to order another copy of Rebuttal to the Rogue, visit www.thewisdomofwomen.net.

If you need a friend who knows the song in your heart, and can sing it back to you when you've forgotten the words, visit my blog at http://malialitman.wordpress.com. If you would like to share your own personal stories involving challenges raising kids, gender discrimination, and general impressions of the book, please let me hear from you. If you just need a good laugh, I will share funnies I receive from you. Let's keep smiling.

Here's to Good Women,
May We Know Them,
May We Be Them,
May We Raise Them.

References

1. Obama, Barack H. "Still Fired Up." New Hampshire Primary. New Hampshire. 08 Jan. 08. Washingtonpost.com. 08 Jan. 08. Washington post. 08 Jan. 08 www.washingtonpost.com/wp-dyn/content/video/2008/01/08/v12008010803937.

2. "Yes We Can Obama Speech." Will.i.am fan site. <http://will.i.am>. Nation Master-Encyclopedia: Yes We Can. www.nationmaster.com/encyclopedia/Yes-We-Can

3. Ibid. en.wikipedia.org/wiki/yes_we_can

4. U.S. Constitution, 19th Amendment.

5. See, e.g. http://www.youtube.com/watch?v=-X6FUwBmclo; http://www.mustsharejokes.com/page/Palin+Debate+Training

6. Kay Bailey Hutchison, Olympia Snowe, Susan Collins, Lisa Murkowski, Elizabeth Dole.

7. Jan Brewer, Arizona; Linda Lingle, Hawaii; M. Jodi Rell, Connecticut.

8. Webster's New World College Dictionary, 4th Edition,2002 at 1242.

9. Id. . at 1287.

10. Id. At 703.

11. Transcript of Vice Presidential Debate, Oct. 2, 2008, New York Times, Election 2008, http://elections.nytimes.com/2008/president/debates/transcripts/vice-presidential-debate

12. Benet, Lorenzo, Trail Blazer, An Intimate Biography of Sarah Palin; See also, Peters, Mike, China Daily, Wherever Palin is going, she won't be going quietly.

13. Ibid.

14. Ibid.

15. Webster's, Id. At 1178.

16. Snow, Kate, ABC News, Politics, Sarah Palin: Why She Resigned, Sarah Palin Talks to ABC News About Why She Resigned.; http://abcnews.go.com/Politics/story?id=8016906&page=1.

17. Sarah Palin has been seen on you tube in her swim suit during a beauty pageant, See, e.g., http:// beltwayblips.dailyradar.com/video/sarah_palin_sw... -

18. http://www.heavy.com/video/sarah-palin-turkey-farm-interview-61405/

19. Federal Judge comments "Put that baby to bed" See e.g., NY Daily News, Manhattan, NY-Federal Judge in Autism Case Blasted Sarah Palin's Use of Her Down Syndrome Child, http://www.vosizneias.com/26943/2009/02/05.

20. Benet, Lorenzo (2009) Trailblazer; an intimate biography of Sarah Palin. 1st Threshold Editions hardcover ed. pg 71,131,155. ISBN-13:978-1-4391-4234-9.

21. Benet Id at 155.

22. Benet Id at 155

23. Newsweek Web Exclusive, Hackers and Spending Sprees. Nov. 5, 2008. www.newsweek.com/id/167581.

24. Vanity Fair, Me and MRS. Palin, Sept. 2, www.vanity fair.com; See also, Tyra Banks interview with Levi Johnson, see http://tyrashow.warnerbros.com/2009/04/levi_johnston.php

25. New York Daily News. Feb. 5, 2009, Manhattan N.Y.-Federal judge in autism case blasted Sarah Palin's Use of Her Down Syndrome Child, http://www.vosizneias.com/26943/2009/02/05/manhattan-ny-federal-judge-in-autism-case.

26. Benet Id at 115.

27. Benet Id at back cover.

28. Associated Press, How Important is McCain's age? July 14,2008, http://www.msnbc.msn.com/id/25671658/

29. Benet Id at 28

30. Benet Id at 45

31. Ibid.

32. Benet Id at 46.

33. Benet Id at 45

34. Benet Id at 46.

35. John McCain graduated 894 out of 899 students at the Naval Academy. See, _Sokolow, Alec, Middie McCain More Moron than Maverick, March 31,2008, http://www.huffingtonpost.com/archive/236/blog/w/alec.

36. Benet Id at 50

37. See, e.g. Dillion, Nancy Reports that Track Palin vandalized school buses aren't true, says pal. Daily News West Coast Bureau, Sept 10, 2008, http://www.nydailynews.com/news/politics/2009/09/10/2008-09-10.

38. Westfall, Sandra Sobieraj, May 15, 2009, Bristol Palin Graduates from High School, http://www.people.com/people/article/0,,20279197,00.html.

39. Fuller, Bonnie, May 21, 2009, Bristol Palin's People Magazine Cover is a Total Promotion for Teen Pregnancy!, http://www.huffington post.com/bonnie-fuller/Bristol-palins-empeopleem/

40. Ibid.

41. "Table 4: Annual Estimates of the Population for Incorporated Places in Alaska, Listed Alphabetically: April 1, 2000 to July 1, 2007" (CSV). 2007 Population Estimates. U.S. Census Bureau, Population Division. June 21, 2006-http://www.census.gov/popest/cities/tables/SUB-EST2007-04-02.csv.

42. White, Rindi. "Palin pressured Wasilla librarian: Gov. Sarah Palin | adn.com." Alaska News, Jobs and Advertising from the Anchorage Daily News | Anchorage, Mat-Su Valley, Kenai Peninsula. 4 Sept. 2008. 27 Feb. 2009 <http://www.adn.com/sarah-palin/story/515512.html>.

43. Sarah Palin can't Name a Newspaper She Reads, http://www.youtube.com/watch?v=xRkWebP2QOY

44. Willhoite, Michael, Daddy's Roomate,1990, ISBN -10: 1-55583118-4 Benet, Lorenzo, Trail Blazer, an intimate biography of Sarah Palin, 2009, Threshold Editions, ISBN-13:978-1-4391-4234-9.a

45. Benet Id at 168

46. Benet Id at 77

47. Ibid.
48. Willhoite, Michael, Daddy's Roommate, Ibid.
49. Ibid.
50. Ibid.
51. Maxwell, Ronald, On Banning Books and Hunting Witches, Sept. 26, 2008, http://www.huffingtonpost.com/ronald-maxwell/on-banning-books-and-hunting_b_129033.html; See Also, MacGillis,Alec, As Mayor of Wasilla, Palin Cut Own Duties, Left Trail of Bad Blood. The Washington Post, Sept 14, 2008, http://www.washingtonpost.com/wp-dyn/content/article/2008/09/13.
52. Ibid
53. Palin's Abuse of Power: Worse Thank you Think., Aug 31, 2008, http://www.huffingtonpost.com/2008/08/31/palins-abuse-of-power.
54. Phillips, Michael. "Palin's Hockey Rink Leads To Legal Trouble in Town She Led - WSJ.com." Business News, Finance News, World, Political & Sports News from The Wall Street Journal - WSJ.com. 6 Sept. 2008. <http://online.wsj.com/article/SB122065537792905483.html>.
55. Ibid
56. Benet, Id at 121.
57. Benet, Id. at 120.
58. Benet, Id. at 121
59. See, Webster Dictionary Fourth Edition, pg. 1077, Peter Principle.
60. Stein, Jonathan, Corn, David, March 12,2009, Mother Jones, Sarah Palin: More Earmark Hypocrisy, http://www.motherjones.com/politics/2009/03/sarah-palin-earmark-hypocrisy.
61. Berton, Hal, Heath, David, The Seattle Times, Palin's earmark requests: more per person than any other state. Sept 2, 2008. http://seattletimes.nwsourcde.com/html/nationworld/2008154532_webpalin02m.html.
62. Ibid.
63. Ibid.
64. Benet, Id. At 108
65. Ibid.
66. Ibid.
67. Stein, Sam, Palin also Supported the "Road to Nowhere" Huffington Post. Sept 4, 2008, http://www.huffingtonpost.com/2008/09/04/palin-also-supported-the_n_123991.html.
68. Benet, Id at 161
69. Ibid.
70. Bridge to Nowhere-Fact Checker, Sept 9http://voices.washingtonpost.com/fact-checker/2008/09/sarah_palin_and_the_bridge_to.html
71. http://www.youtube.com/watch?v=NWxhDpX8IZs
72. "Sarah Palin RNC Convention Speech (VIDEO) (TEXT)." Breaking News and Opinion on The Huffington Post. 3 Sept. 2008.

141

<http://www.huffingtonpost.com/2008/09/03/sarah-palin-rnc-conventio_n_123703.html>.

73. Hayasaki, Erika, Palin said yes to a road to nowhere, Los Angeles Times, Sept 19, 2008, http://articles.latimes.com/2008/sep/19/nation/na-bridge; See also, Stein, Ibid

74. Ibid

75. Stein, Ibid.

76. Stein, Ibid.

77. Ibid.

78. Ibid

79. http://siu.blogs.cnn.com/2008/09/23/road-to-nowhere. CNN special investigations unit Sept 23, 2008.

80. CNN Politics.com; http://www.cnn.com/2008/politics/09/24/palin.road.to.nowhere/indes.htm. The bridge failed but the "Road to Nowhere" was built.

81. Ibid

82. www.samefacts.com/archives/cnn_nowhere_culdes...; www.samefacts.com/archives/palin_/2008/09/gov...

83. Branchflower, Stephen (October 10, 2008). "Stephen Branchflower report to the Legislative Council" (PDF). State of Alaska Legislature http://download2.legis.state.ak.us/DOWNLOAD.pdf.

84. Branchflower, Stephen (October 10, 2008). "Stephen Branchflower report to the Legislative Council" (PDF). State of Alaska Legislature.http://download2.legis.state.ak.us/DOWNLOAD.pdf.

85. Van der Galien, Michael, Poligazette, Meghan McCain won't say whether she will support Palin in 2012 April 10, 2009 http://www.poligazette.com/2009/04/10; See also, 23/6 Huffington Post, Why won't Megan talk about Sarah Palin? http://www.huffingtonpost.com/archive/236/news/2009/01/12/poll.

86. MSNBC, Levi Johnston's mom arrested on drug charges, Oct. 14, 2008, http://www.msnbc.msn.com/id/28313509; See also, Hollander, Zaz, Anchorage Daily News, April 3, 2009, Todd Palin's half sister is arrested for burglary(Caught by an armed homeowner)., http://www.freerepublic.com/focus/news/2222105.

87. Associated Press, Oct. 21, 2008, Alaska governor Sarah Palin charged the state for her children to travel with her, including to events where they were not invited,…the charges included $21,012.00 for her three daughters ' 64 one way and 12 round-trip commercial flights since she took office in Dec. 2006…http://www.msnbc.msn.com/id/27310999/

88. See e.g. www.youtube.com/watch?v=iwkb9_zB2Pg-99k; Blumenthal, Max, The Witch hunter Anoints Sarah Palin, Sept. 24, 2008, The Witch Hunter Anoints Sarah Palin, http://www.huffingtonpost.com/max-blumenthal/the-witch-hunter-anoints_b_128805.html.

89. See, Vanity fair, Id; www.youtube.com/watch?v=URIypadx3nO, Hockey Moms Against Sarah Palin., See also, Sarah Palin in spotlight:"

Average Hockey Mom' Sept 3, 2008, abcnews.go.com/politics/conventions/story?id=5718030.

90. Ibid.

91. http://www.huffingtonpost.com/2008/10/06/olbermann-special-comment_n_132456.html.

92. See, http://www.youtube.com/watch?v=NWxhDpX8IZse,

93. Ibid.

94. Kilkenny, Anne, About Sarah Palin: an e-mail from Wasilla, Sept 2, 2008, Crosscut, http://crosscut.com/2008/09/02/2008-election/17341.

95. Ibid.

96. Benet, Id. at 55-57.

97. Benet, Id at 181

98. Franke-Ruta, Garance, Palin Says she Weighed Abortion, The Washington Post, April 18, 2009.http://www.washingtonpost.com/wpdyn/content/article/2009/04/17/AR2009041703184.ht.

99. Benet, Id at 182. Sarah kept the pregnancy a secret for 5 months 181. She couldn't talk about it.

100. Benet, Id at 185-186.

101. Certainly, at least one blog, authored by a medical doctor has made a persuasive argument that Trig was not Sarah's child, but Bristol's baby. See, http://www.palindeception.com/index.html.

102. Ibid.

103. Murray, Mark, Bristol Palin pregnant—right now, Sept 1, 2008; http://firstread.msnbc.msn.com/archive/2008/09/01/1318541.aspx.

104. Associated Press, Bristol Palin Says Abstinence "Not Realistic at All," Feb. 18. 2009 hyyp://www.foxnews.com/story/0,2933,495244,00.html.

105. Landau, Elizabeth, CNN, Report: Teen pregnancies up for the first time in 15 years, July 11,2008, http://www.cnn.com/2008/health/07/10/teen.pregnancy/indes.html

106. Ibid.

107. Tanner, Lindsey, Nearly 1 in 4 Teen Girls has a STD, CDC Says, ABC News, March 11, 2008, http://abcnews.go.com/health/reproductive health/story?id=4429246&page=1

108. Inside Cover, Levi Johnston, Palin Trade Barbs Over Resignation, July 10, 2009, http://www.newsmax.com/insidecover/johnston_palin_resogm2009/07/10/234075.html?.

109. Benet, Id at 110-111.

110. Benet, Id at 127

111. Castina, Bristol Palin Baby Pictures, People Magazine (Tripp Photos $300,000) http://www.popcrunch.com/bristol-palin-baby-pictures-people-magazine-tto[[-photos-300000; See also, Drudge Rept, Magazine Pays $300,000 for Palin Baby Pictures, http:// www.drudge.com/archive/116268/magazine-pays-300000-palin-baby-picture/

112. See e.g. Tresniowski, Alex, People Magazine, Sarah Palin's sister-in-law Arrested for Burglary, April 4, 2009, http://www.people.com/people/article/0,,20270168,00.html; Celebrity News, April 9, 2009, Levi Johnston's Mom "Beggin " Palin family not to

Keep Tripp From Them,
http://www.usmagazine.com/news/levi-johnstons-mom-begging-palin-f
amily-not-to-keep-tr (Sherry, who faces six felony counts of possessing
and selling prescription painkiller oxycontin).

113. Benet, Id at 203

114. New York Daily News, Dec. 16, 2008,McCain Refuses to Endorse Palin
for President in 2012: 'I can't'. www.nydailynews.com/news/poli-
tics/2008/12/15/2008

115. Van Der Galien, Michael, Meghan McCain won't say whether she will
support Palin in 2012, April 10, 2009,
http://www.poligazette.com/2009/04/10/meghan-mccain-wont-say-whet
her - she-will -support.

116. Newsweek, Nov. 5, 2008, Hackers and Spending Sprees, Highlights from
Newsweek's special election project.
http://www.newsweek.com/id/167581.

117. See, Fact Check.org.,
http://www.factcheck.org/skfactcheck/if_a_vice_president_assumes_the_
presidency.html.April 10, 2008 (If the president dies, and the VP is
sworn in as the new pres., the new president appoints someone to fill
her or his old position …subject to congressional approval).See also, 25th
Amendment: Whenever there is a vacancy in the office of the Vice President, the President shall nominate a Vice President who shall take office
upon confirmation by a majority vote of both Houses of Congress.)

118. Chris Matthews scoffs at Sarah Palin, http://www.polit-
ico.com/news/stories/0509/22491.html

119. Sarah Palin's Ghostwriter Problem Discussed on 'Meet the Press'| Sun,
Oct 4, 2009 , Rachel Maddow, Meet the Press. See,
http://littlegreenfootballs.com/article/34824_Sa-
rah_Palins_Ghostwriter_Problem_Discussed_on_Meet_the_Press

120. Benet, Id at 23.

121. Benet, Id at 168 (one minister of the church suggested that supporters of
John Kerry in the 2004 presidential election would never get to heaven).

122. Cooper, Michael, Alaskan Is McCain's Choice; First Woman on G.O.P.
Ticket, August, 29, 2008. www.nytimes.com/2008/08/30/us/poli-
tics/29palin.html?hp

123. West, Darrell, The Post Convention Bump, Sept. 02, 2008,
http://brookings.feedroom.com/?fr_story. The Brookings Institution.
Vice President Governance Studies

124. Brown, Adriane, McCain Camp to Ifill: Go Easy on Palin. Sept 29, 2008,
Huffington Post,
www.huffingtonpost.com/2008/09/29/mccain-camp-to-ifill-go-e-n

125. Women on the Web, http://www.wowowow.com/post/3 reasons why
some women hate sarah palin, Oct. 3, 2008; See also, Luscombe,
Belinda Time 2008.

126. Couric, Katie, One-on-One with Sarah Palin, Sept 24, 2008,
www.cbsnews.com/stories/2008/09/24/ eveningnews/main. See also,
www.youtube.com/watch?v=vbg6hF0nShQ CBS Sarah Palin Interview.

127. Ibid

128. Griffin, Drew, and Kathleen Johnston, CNN politics.com, July 7, 2009, Palin:"I am not a quitter; I am a fighter" http://edi-tion.cnn.com/2009/POLITis/07/07/palin.resignation.

129. Ibid.

130. Ibid.

131. Ibid.

132. Ibid.

133. Ibid.

134. At state level, GOP, Dems learn to get along - USATODAY.com; http://www.alaskajournal.com/stories/110407/hom_20071104035.shtml ; Rasmussen Reports™: The Most Comprehensive Public Opinion Data Anywhere ; ^ Rasmussen, "New poll shows slump in Palin's popularity among Alaskans." Miami Herald. 7 May 2009. http://www.miamiherald.com/515/story/1035915.html.

135. Griffin Ibid.

136. 480 Purdum, Todd, Vanity Fair, August 2009, http://www.vanityfair.com /politics/features/2009/08/sarah-palin200908? at 2.

137. D'Oro, Rachel, Associated Press, Palin resigns as governor, leaves plans secret, July 3, 2009., http://news.yahoo.com/s/ap/20090703/ap_on_re_us/us_palin_resigning.

138. Associated Press, Inside Cover, July 10, 2009, Levi Johnston, Palin Trade Barbs Over Resignation, http://www.newsmax.com/insidecover/johnston_palin_resign/2009/07/10 /234075.html. See also Vanity Fair, Ibid.

139. Silva, Mark, Sarah Palin's book deal:$11 million?, The Swamp, Jan. 22, 2009, http://www.swamppoliticds.com/news/politics/blog/2009/01.

140. Nasaw, Daniel, Oct. 27, 2009, Sarah Palin earned $1.25 m advance for Going Rogue memoir, guardian.co.uk, http:www.guard-ian.co.uk/world/2009/oct 27/sarah-palin-book-deal-harpercollins.

141. Ibid.

142. Sarah Palin Biography, July 7, 2009, http://www.biography.com/arti-cles/Sarah-Palin-360398.

143. Sarah Palin's Experience, http://www.linkedin.com/pub/sa-rah-palin/11/292/3a1.

144. See, Charlie Gibson Interview, Sept. 11, 2008, www.youtube.com/watch?v=EqxDbAwvBhy; See also, US Magazine, Sept 11,2008, Sarah Palin "Didn't Blink" when offered the VP Nomina-tion. http:// www.usmagazine.com/news/sa-rah-palin-didnt-blink-when-offered-the-vice-president.

145. Office of Alaska Governor Sarah Palin, http://www.gov.state.ak.us/proclamations.php?id=1900, May 15,2009.

146. Simon, Roger, The Sins of Sarah Palin, Yahoo News, July 7, 2009, http://news.yahoo.com/s/politico/20090707/ pl_pollitico.

147. Benet, Ibid.

148. Ibid.

149. See, e.g., Nasaw, Id.

150. See, http://webcenter.polls.aol.com/modular.jsp?resType=7, 9-20-09 out of 151,302 people voting 43% of those responsing identified Sarah Palin as the worst GOP presidential candidate for 2012. The first runner up was Ron Paul with only 16% of the votes cast.

151. Vanity Fair, Me and MRS. Palin, Sept. 2, www.vanity fair.com; See also, Tyra Banks interview with Levi Johnson, see http://tyrashow.warnerbros.com/2009/04/levi_johnston.php

152. CBS News, Transcript : Palin and McCain Interview, Ibid.

153. Ibid.

154. Ibid.

155. Ibid.

156. Ibid.

157. CBS , One on One with Sarah Palin, Sept. 24, 2008 by Katie Couric, http://www.cbsnews.com/stories/2008/09/24/eveningnews/main4476 173,shtml

158. http://www.youtube.com/watch?v=L8__aXxXPVc&NR=1(Cafferty file)

159. Ibid.

160. Ibid

161. Katie Couric Interview: Transcript, http://tv.spreadit.org/sarah-palin-katie -couric-interview palin

162. Ibid.

163. Vanity Fair, Me and Mrs. Palin, Sept. 2, 2009, www.vanityfair.com

164. Ibid.

165. Sarah Palin Katie Couric Interview: Palin Couric Interview Transcript; http://tv.spreadit.org/sarah-palin-katie-couric-interviewpalin-couric-in-terview-transcript.

166. Beat Crazy: William Shatner's Sarah Palin (transcript included), Wed. July 29,2009; http://mensnewsdaily.com/sexandmetro/2009/07/29/beat-crazy-wil-liam-shatners-sarah.

167. The Amazing Palin-Dobson Interview, Wed. Oct. 22,2008, http://blog.beliefnet.com/stevenwalldman/2008.10.the-amaz-ing-palindobson-interv.html.

168. Weiner, Rachel, Palin Claimed Dinosaurs and People Coexisted, Huffington Post, 9-28-08, http://www.huffingtonpost.com/2008/09/28/palin-claimed-dinosaurs-a

169. Ibid.; www.youtube.com/watch?v=C6urw_PWHYk - 167k http://www.youtube.com/watch?v=C6urw_PWHYk&NR=1&fea-ture=fvwp;

170. Ibid.

171. www.cbsnews.com/stories/2008/10/01/eveningnews/m... - 119k; see also, Los Angeles Times, Katie Couric's Supreme Court Questions stump Sa-rah Palin, http://latimesblogs.latimes.com/washing-ton/2008/10/palin-couric.html.

172. Newton-Small, Jay Time Interview, Transcript:TIME'S interview with Sarah Palin, Aug. 29, 2008,http://www.time.com/time/nation/arti-cle/085991837536-100.html.

173. Vanity Fair, Me and Mrs. Palin, Sept. 2, 2009, www.vanityfair.com

174. Transcript: The Vice Presidential Debate, Oct. 2, 2008, http://elections.nytimes.com/2008/president/debates/transcripts/vice-presidential-debate/

175. Ibid.

176. Ibid.

177. Ibid.

178. Ibid.

179. Ibid.

180. Ibid.

181. Vanity Fair , Me and Mrs. Palin, Sept. 2, 2009, www.vanityfair.com

182. Ibid.

183. Ibid.

184. Ibid.

185. Ibid.

186. Ibid.

187. Ibid.

188. Ibid.

189. Ibid.

190. Ibid.

191. Stein, Sam, 9-1-08, Palin On Abortion: I'd Oppose Even if My own Daughter was raped, http://www.huffingtonpost.com/2008/09/01/palin-on-abortion-id-oppo

192. Ibid.

193. The Amazing Palin-Dobson Interview, Oct. 22, 2008; http://blog.beliefnet.com/stevewaldman/2008/10/the-amazing-palindobson-interv.html.

194. Vanity Fair, Me and Mrs. Palin. Id.

195. Franke-Ruta, Garance, The Washington Post, Palin Says She Weighed Abortion, April 18, 2009; http://www.washingtonpost.com/wp-dyn/content/article/2009/04/17/AR200904/17/AR2009041703184.

196. Primm, Katie, Murray, Mark, MSNBC First Read, Sept. 1, 2008, http://firstread.msnbc.msn.com/archive/2008/09/01/1320417.aspx.

197. CNN, Bristol Palin:Abstinence for all teens "not realistic.," http://www.cnn.com/2009/POLITICS/02/17/bristol.palin.interview.

198. Star News on line, http://forums.starnewsonline.com/eve/forums/a/tpc/f/5731000496/m/6761073628.

199. Griffin, Drew, Johnston, Kathleen, Palin:"I'm not a quitter; I am a fighter." Cnn Politics.com, http://www.cnn.com/2009/POLITICS/07/07/palin .resignation/indes.html.

200. Peters, Mike, Wherever Palin's going, she won't be going quietly.http://www.chinadaily.com.cn/world/2009-07-28/content_8481103.htm

201. Ibid.

202. CBS News, Transcript:Palin and McCain Interview, Sept. 30, 2008, More in-Depth Answers to Questions Katie Couric Asked McCain and Palin

on the Broadcast; http://www.cbsnews.com/stories/2008/09/30/eveningnews/main4490788.shtml?source=m.

203. Ensler, Eve, Drill, Drill, Drill, Sept. 8, 2008; http://www.huffingtonpost.com/eve-ensler/drill-drill-drill_b_124829.html

204. Benet, Id.

205. Vanity Fair, Me and Mrs. Palin, Id.

206. Obama, Barack, 1-18-09, Parade , www.parade.com/export/sites/default/news/2009/01/barack-obama-letter-to-my-daughters

207. Huffington Post, Obama: As A Woman, Michelle Had to Make Sacrifices I Didn't Have To. Oct. 22,2009.

208. Friedan, Betty, The Feminine Mystique, , W.W. Norton & Company Ltd., 1997,1991, 1974, 1963, ISBN 0-393-32257-2pbk.

209. Ibid.

210. Id at 41

211. Sullivan, Ibid

212. Ibid.

213. See e.g., Humm, Maggie (1990) The dictionary of feminist theory. Columbus:hio State University Press. Pg. 278. ISBN 0-8142-0506-2.; Walker, Rebecca (1992) Becoming the Third Wave, Ms. (January/February, 1992) 39-41; Krolokke, Charlotte; Anne Scott Sorensen (2005). "Three Waves of Feminism: From Suffragettes to Girls" Gender Communication Theories and Analyses: From Silence to Performance. Sage.pg. 24.ISBN 0761929185.

214. Encyclopaedia Britanica's Guide to Women's History, Timeline: Through the Centuries. http://search.eb.com/women/timeline?tocID=9404138&section=249219

215. Bazelon, Emily,The Mother of Feminism, New York Times, Dec.31, 2006/ http://www.nytimes.com/2006/12/31

216. Ibid

217. Friedman, Id at 41.

218. Stein, Sam, Palin on Abortion: I'd Oppose Abortion even if my own Daughter was Raped. http://www.huffingtonpost.com/2008/09/01/palin-on-abortion-id-oppo_n_122924.html

219. Dilanian, Ken, Kelley, Matt, USA Today, 9-11-08 Palin's town used to bill victims for rape kits. http://www.usatoday.com/news/politics/election2008/2008-09-10-rape-exams_N.htm

220. Primm, Katie, Murray , Mark, MSNBC, http://firstread.msnbc.msn.com/archive/2008/09/01/1320417.aspx

221. Tsunami Warning Sign, US Geological Survey.

222. Benet, Ibid.

223. Jefferson, Thomas. "The Declaration of Independence," 1776

224. Ibid

225. www.nps.gov/archive/wori/address.htm; "The Seneca Falls Convention (July 19, 1848)."

REFERENCES

226. Ibid; Kelly, Martin. "Seneca Falls Convention," About.com, American History, Seneca Falls Convention, Background and Details, http://american history.about.com/od/womenssuffrage/a/senecafalls.htm

227. Photo Library of Congress, memory.loc.gov. /.../3a02000/3a02500/ 3a02558r.jpg

228. Linder, Doug , The Trial of Susan B. Anthony for Illegal Voting, 2001, http;//www.law.umkc.edu/faculty/projects/ftrials/An- thony/sbaaccount.html.

229. Ibid.

230. Susan B. Anthony Speech-After Being Convicted of Voting, http://www.famous-speeches-and-speech-topics.info/famous -speeches-by-women/

231. Harvey, Sheridan, Marching for the vote, Remembering the Women Suffrage Parade "Marching for the vote." Library of Congress, Informa- tion Bulletin, March 1998 http://www.loc.gov/loc/lcib/9803/suffrage.html.

232. Photo Library of Congress, Digital ID : cph 3a02913, http:/mem- ory.loc.gov/cgi-bin/query.

233. Adams, Katherine, Alice Paul and the American Suffrage Campaign,2008 ISBN 978-0-252-074771-4 University of Illinois Press.

234. U.S. Constitution-Amendment 19; http://www.usconstitution.net/xconst_Am19.html.; See also, "19th Amendment to the U.S. Constitution: Women's Right to Vote (1920)."

235. Hamilton, Geoff. "The Mary Tyler Moore Show." The Museum of Broadcast Communications. http://www/museum.tv/ar- chives/etv/M/htmlM/marytylermo/marytylermo.htm.

236. "Roe v. Wade, 410 U.S. 113 (1973)." FindLaw: Cases and Codes. <http://caselaw.lp.findlaw.com/scripts/getcase.pl?navby=CASE&court= US&vol=410&page=113>.

237. Ibid

238. Branigin, William, Fred Barbash and Dela Deane, Washington Post, July 1, 2005, http://www.washingtonpost.com.

239. Ledbetter v. Goodyear Tire & Rubber Co., 550 U.S. 618 (2007)-." Wikipedia, the free encyclopedia. <http://en.wikipedia.org/wiki/Ledbetter_v._Goodyear_Tire_&_Rub- ber_Co.>.

240. Ibid

241. Ibid

242. Litman, Malia, *Rebuttal to the Rogue,* 2009.

243. Middleton, Ken, Middle Tennessee State Univ. Library, American Women Through Time, http://frank.mtsu.edu/_kmiddlet/history/women/time/wh-recent.html; See also, Encyclopaedia Britannica's Guide to Women's History, 300 Women who changed the World, http://search.eb.com/women/time?tocId=9404138&section=249219; Margaret Thatcher, 10 Downing Street, Official Site of the Prime Minis- ter's Office, www/number 10.gov.uk.

244. Zimon, Jill Miller, Obama Creates Council on Women and Girls, Mr. 11,2009, The Moderate Voice, http://themoderatevoice.com.

245. Weiner, Rachel, The Huffington Post Jan. 27, 2009, Lilly Ledbetter Act: Obama Signs His First Bill, http://www.huffingtonpost.com/2009/01/27/lily-ledbetter-act

246. Transcript of Obama-Sotomayor announcement, May 26, 2009, CNN Politics.com, http://www.cnn.com/2009/POLITICS/05/26/obama.sotomayor.tran-script/index.html.

247. Ten Things About Judge Sonia Sotomayor, May 26, 2009, http://webmail.aol.com/42951/aol/en-us. Move On .org, Political Ac-tion<moveon-help@list.moveon.org.

248. Transcript of Obama-Sontomayor announcement, Id.

249. Ibid.

250. Ibid.

251. Alexander,Goldwin, Wallet Pop, Government Programs put college De-grees in Reach for Moms, June 16, 2009, http;//www.walletpop.com/col-lege-finance/eim/_a/bbdp/government-programs-put-college…6/16/2009.

252. Ibid.

253. Ibid.

254. Benen, Steve, Sonia Sotomayor Wins Confirmation 68-31, Political Ani-mal, Aug. 6, 2009, http://www.washingtonmonthly.com/archives/indi-vidual/2009.

255. Ibid.

256. Ibid.

257. Obama presents 16 with Presidential Medal of Freedom. Aug, 12, 2009, http://www.cnn.com/2009/POLITICS/08/12/medal.of.freedom.

258. www.biography.com/featured-biography; John McCain; see also, Wikipedia.org/wiki/john_mcCain. Six-packs, automatic transmissions and the American Express Card were all introduced after he was born. McCain jokes that he is "older than dirt." Associated Press, July 14, 2008, How important is McCain's age? http://www.msnbc.msn.com/id/25671658/.

259. Associated Press, How important is McCain's age? July 14, 2008, http://www.msnbc.msn.com/id/25671658.

260. http://www.nydailynews.com/gossip/2008/06/10.

261. MSNBC.com's First Read,MSNBC Morning Joe uncritically reported Palin's misquote of Albright,ignored Albright's explanation of her re-marks, Oct. 6, 2008. Media Matters, http://mediamatters.org/research/200810060005. See also, Pittney Nico, Palin Misquotes Albright: "Place in Hell Reserved For Women Who Don't Support other Women." Oct. 5, 2008. www.huffingtonpost.com/2008/10/05/palin-mis-quotes-albright.m.131967.html

262. Not surprisingly, John McCain was one of the Senators who opposed the appointment of Judge Sonia Sotomayor, as the third woman Justice of the United States Supreme Court.

263. Cnn Politics, Clinton wins key primaries, Cnn projects; McCain clinches nod, March 5, 2008, www.cnn.com/2008/POLITICS/03/04/arch.4.con-tests/indes.html.

REFERENCES

264. http://mccainkeatingfive.com/?page_id=19, What is the Keating Five? One Crook Went to Prison, The Other is Running for President.

265. Ledbetter, Id

266. http:// www.nydailynews.com/gossip/2008/06/10/

267. Ibid; See also, Wikipedia.org/wiki/john_mcCain

268. www.biography.com/featured-biography; John McCain; see also, Wikipedia.org/wiki/john_mcCain

269. Ibid

270. Ibid

271. Ibid

272. Ibid

273. Ibid

274. Lewison, Jed, Jed Report, CNN Talks with McCain about his extramarital Affairs. Aug. 21,2008, www.jedreport.com/2008/08/cnn-talks-with-html.

275. Lowen, Linda, Profile of Cindy McCain, Wife of Presidential Candidate John McCain, Aug. 8, 2008; http://womensissues.about.com/od/influentialwomen/p/CindyMcCain.htm., see also, Wikipedia.org/wiki/john_McCain.

276. Ibid

277. Ibid

278. Ibid

279. Ibid

280. Ibid

281. Schecter, Cliff, The Real McCain: Why Conservatives Don't Trust Him, and Why Independents Shouldn't. See also, Savan, Leslie, Augus 8, 2008, A Mad Men cameo for John McCain? (re-telling McCain's gender jokes, including an ape-rape joke, and the time he volunteered Cindy for a beauty pageant at a biker rally"…I told her with a little luck she could be the only woman to serve as both the first lady and Miss Buffalo Chip") www.guardian.co.uk/commentisfree/2008/aug/08/johnmccain.gender?gusrc.

282. www.youngturks.com. May 2, 2008; see also, Juliano, Nick, Report:McCain's Profane Tirade at his Wife. April 7,2008, www.huffingtonpost.com/2008/04/07/report-mccains-profane-tirade, See also, www.biography.com/featured-biography/john-mccain bio.true story

283. Stein, Sam, Mc"Cain Ape Rape Joke Recalled By Sources, July 15, 2008, www.huffingtonpost.com/2008/07/15sources recall mccains joke.

284. Brownielocks, 2004, Miss America Pageant History & Cartoon Fun. http://www.brownielocks.com/americapageant.html.

285. Ibid

286. Library of Congress-photo archives—Miss America.1921.

287. Ibid

288. Ibid

289. Ibid

290. Ibid

291. Ibid

292. Ibid

293. Ibid

294. www.youtube.com/watch?v=lj3inxz8Dww. Miss Teen USA 2007-South Carolina

295. Miss South Carolina v. Sarah Palin on Foreign Policy: Who is the More Articulate Spokesperson for America to the World? http://santitafarella.wordpress.com/2008/09/11/miss-south-carolina-v-sarah-palin-on-foreign

296. AP, USA Today, 1-26-08, Miss Michigan crowned Miss America 2008, www.usatoday.com/life/people/2008-1-26-missamerica-2008

297. Sex in Las Vegas, www.usatourist.com/english/places/lasvegas/sex.; Diggers Realm, Prostitution Legal in Rhode Island. www.diggersrealm.com/mt/archives/001203.html.

298. Saad, Lydia, Americans Predict Obama Will be Next U.S. President, June 16, 2008; http://www.gallup.com/poll/107995/americans-predict-obama-will-next-us-president.

299. Ibid.

300. Ibid.

301. "Election Center 2008 - Election Results & Politics News from CNN.com." CNN.com - Breaking News, U.S., World, Weather, Entertainment & Video News. http://www.cnn.com/elections>.

302. Ibid

303. Ibid

304. Ibid

305. Ibid

306. Ibid

307. Institute for Women's Policy Research. "Women's Vote Clinches Election Victory: 8 Million More Women than Men Voted for Obama...American Women Make Their V." Press release. 07 Nov. 08. See also, Center for American Women and Politics. <http://www.cawp.rutgers.edu>.

308. Carroll, Id. at 71,76.; See also, Tolleson-Rinehart, Sue, Josephson, Jyl J., Gender and American Politics, Sharpe, 2005, ISBN 0-7656-1569-X.

309. Institute for Women's Policy Research. "Women's Vote Clinches Election Victory: 8 Million More Women than Men Voted for Obama...American Women Make Their V." Press release. 07 Nov. 08. See also, Center for American Women and Politics. <http://www.cawp.rutgers.edu>.

310. Ibid

311. Ibid

312. Ibid

313. Ibid

314. Conason, Joe, Aug. 30, 2008, McCain's Palin pick is the epitome of tokenism. Salon.com, Aug. 30, 2008. www.salon.com/opinion/conason/2008.

315. U.S. Census Bureau News, U.S. Department of Commerce, Washington D.C.; One-Third of Young Women Have Bachelor's Degrees, Robert

Bernstein, Jan 10, 2008. www.census.gov/Press -Release/www/re-leases/archives/education/011106.

316. U.S. Census Bureau, Facts for Features, June 14, 2007. www.census.gov/Press-Release/www/releases/archives/facts_for_features_special

317. Jones, Mother, June 11, 2008 Huffington Post, McCain Admits He Doesn't Know How to Use a Computer. www.huffingtonpost.com/2008/06/11.

318. Sarah Palin Exposed. McCain only Met Palin Once Before He Offered Palin VP Nomination.www.Sarahpalinexposed.com

319. Gallup Daily Tracking Poll

320. Gallup Poll 2008.

321. Institute for Women's Policy Research. "Women's Vote Clinches Election Victory: 8 Million More Women than Men Voted for Obama...American Women Make Their V." Press release. 07 Nov. 08.

322. Ledbetter v. Goodyear Tire & Rubber Co., 550 U.S. 618(2007).

323. John McCain supports Wage Discrimination, www.feministing.com/archives/009085

324. Institute for Women's Policy Research. "Women's Vote Clinches Election Victory: 8 Million More Women than Men Voted for Obama...American Women Make Their V." Press release. 07 Nov. 08.

325. Ibid.; See also, Institute for Women's Policy Research. "Women's Vote Clinches Election Victory: 8 Million More Women than Men Voted for Obama...American Women Make Their V." Press release. 07 Nov. 08. See also, Center for American Women and Politics. <http://www.cawp.rutgers.edu>. 08 Feb. 2009 <http://huffingtonpost.com/2008/7/24/obama-in-berlin>.

326. www.BarackObama.com

327. Ibid

328. Ibid

329. Ibid

330. Witter, Lisa. The She Spot. San francisco: Berrett-KoehlerInc., 08.

331. Mullins, Brody. Women Heavily Favor Obama in Donations. Sept 23, 2008. Wall Street Journal on line, //online.wsj.com/article/SB122213281072465941.

332. Ibid

333. Parsons, Christi. "Barack's Rock: Michelle Obama." 22 Apr. 07. Chicago Tribune.

334. Obama, Barack. The Audacity of Hope. New York: Crown Group, 06.

335. Ibid

336. Obama, Barack H. "Still Fired Up." New Hampshire Primary. New Hampshire. 08 Jan. 08. Washingtonpost.com. 08 Jan. 08. Washington post. 08 Jan. 08 www.washingtonpost.com/wp-dyn/content/video/2008/01/08/v12008010803937

337. Ibid

338. "Yes We Can Obama Speech." Will.i.am fan site. <http://will.i.am>. Nation Master-Encyclopedia: Yes We Can.
www.nationmaster.com/encyclopedia/Yes-We-Can

339. en.wikipedia.org/wiki/yes_we_can

340. "Sarah Palin: Former Beauty Queen, Future vp?" 29 Aug. 08.

341. Kizzia, Tom. ":Creation science" enters the race." Anchorage Daily News [Anchorage Alaska] 27 Oct. 06.

342. Lowen, Linda, About.com, Impact of the Women's Vote in the 2008 Election; http://womensissues.about.com/of/womensissuesin2008race/a/WomenVote2008.htm.

343. Ibid.

344. Ibid.

345. Ibid.

346. Hornick, Ed, Costello, Carol, Will her gender sway women to Palin? Cnn Politics.com Sept. 3, 2008; http:??
www.cnn.com/2008/POLITICS/09/02/palin.women/indes.html.

347. Ibid.

348. Ibid.

349. Ibid.

350. Ibid.

351. Pear, Robert, New York Times, Average Size of Household in U.S. Declines to Lowest Ever Recorded, april 1987,
http://www.nytimes.com/1987/04/15/us/average-size-of-house-hold-in-us-declines-to-low.

352. U.S. Census Bureau , Census 2000 Summary File 1 (SF 1) 100 – percent data, Tables P34"family type by presence and age of own children, Table ST-F1-2000 Sept 15, 2004

353. Ibid.

354. The Shriver Report, A Woman's Nation, at 129.

355. Erb, Bonnie, The Numbers in Hillary's Favor, U.S. News & World Report, April 2, 2008, www.usnews.com/blogs/erbe/2008/4/2.

356. Slater, Wayne, Many Obama voters ignored other Texas primary races, Dallas Morning News, March 9, 2008.
www.dallasnews.com/sharedcontent/dws/ds/latestnews/stories

357. Institute for Women's Policy Research. "Women's Vote Clinches Election Victory: 8 Million More Women than Men Voted for Obama...American Women Make Their V." Press release. 07 Nov. 08.

358. Reuters, www.telegraph.co.uk/news/2592704/Prepare-for-...

359. Rossi, Rosalind (January 20, 2007). "The woman behind Obama." Chicago Sun-Times .
http://www.suntimes.com/news/metro/221458,CST-NWS-mich21.article. Retrieved on 2008-01-22. The Trustees of Princeton University. 2008
http://www.princeton.edu/main/academics/departments/. Retrieved on 2008-05-18.See also, Ressner, Jeffrey, 2-22-08, Michelle Obama thesis was on racial divide. www.politico.com/news/stories/

360. Brown, Sarah (December 7, 2005). "Obama '85 Masters Balancing Act". *Daily Princetonian*
http://www.dailyprincetonian.com/archives/2005/12/07/news/14049.shtm l., See also, Lowen, Linda, Profile of Michelle Obama About.com Women's Is-
sues.womensissues.about.com/of/influentialwomen/p/MichelleObama.htm

361. Lowen, Linda , First Lady Michelle Obama Will be a Stay at Home Mom First-Good or Bad?,
womensissues.about.com/b/2008/11/10/first-lady-michelle-obama

362. The Power of Oprah to Help Obama,
www.marginalrevolution.com/marginalrevolution/2008. The Role of Celebrity Endorsements in Politics: Oprah, Obama, and 2008 Democratic Primary, Sept 08.

363. Ibid

364. Lowen, Linda. Oprah Tops Forbes List of World's Most Powerful Celebrities, June 12, 2008, womenissues.about.com/b/2008/06/12/oprah tops forbes list of worlds most powerful women

365. Borer, Elizabeth, Oprah One of Forbes Most Powerful Women, Aug. 28, 2008, www.oprah.about.com/b/2008/08/28. See also, womenissues.about.com/od/oprahwinfre1/oprah Winfrey Talk Show Host One, Oprah Winfrey-Talk Show Host One of World's Most Influential Women.

366. Allen-Mills,Tony, Times Online, Women turn on 'traitor' Oprah Winfrey for backing Barack Obama. Oprah fans leave a barrage of negative messages on her official website in response to the talk show host's support of Obama. www.timesonline.co.uk/tol/news/world/us, Jan. 20, 2008.

367. Ibid

368. Ibid

369. Ibid. See also,Martelle, Scott, State's First Landy is for Obama, Los Angeles Times, Feb. 4, 2008, articles.latimes.com/2008/feb/04/nation

370. Ibid;http://www.youtube.com/watch?v=VJAlngPvbkg

371. www.californiawomen.org; We Empower Women to be Architects of Change; See also, Martelle, Scott, State's First Landy is for Obama, Los Angeles Times, Feb. 4,2008, articles.latimes.com/2008/feb/04/nation

372. Martelle, Id

373. www.californiawomen.org.

374. Martin, Roland. "California First Lady Maria Shriver endorses Obama." 04 Feb. 08; Rosenthal, Andrew, Michelle, Maria, Caroline and Oprah on rhw Huarinfa in California , New York Times Feb. 4, 2008, www.nytimes.com/2008/02/04

375. Martin, Roland. "California First Lady Maria Shriver endorses Obama." 04 Feb. 08

376. www.Youtube-LA Rally; Maria Shriver Announces Her Support for Barack Obama, Feb. 3, 2008;
www.youtube.com/watch?v=62_ajokkuHA.

377. Johnson, Jone. "Caroline Kennedy." About.com Women's History; See also, http://www.youtube.com/watch?v=ltbpoYT8LVY.

378. Kennedy, Caroline. "A President Like My Father." The New York Times. 27 Jan. 2008. <http://www.nytimes.com/2008/01/27/opinion/27kennedy.html?hp>.

379. Kenney, Caroline. "A President Like My Father." The New York Times. 27 Jan. 2008. <http://www.nytimes.com/2008/01/27/opinion/27kennedy.html?hp>.

380. Ibid.

381. Abcarian, Robin. "Obama gets major labor endorsement - Los Angeles Times." Los Angeles Times - News from Los Angeles, California and the World. 16 Jan. 2008. <http://www.latimes.com/news/politics/la-na-labor16jan16,0,656548.story?coll=la-home-center>.

382. "California Democratic Delegation 2008". thegreenpapers.com
http://www.thegreenpapers.com/P08/CA-D.phtml
Ibid., See also, Abcarioan Id.

383. Eisenhower, Susan. "Susan Eisenhower - Why I'm Backing Obama - washingtonpost.com." Washingtonpost.com - nation, world, technology and Washington area news and headlines. 2 Feb. 2008.
http://www.washingtonpost.com/wp-dyn/content/article/2008/02/01/AR2008020102621.html; See also, Biography of Susan Eisenhower. – Save America's Treasures

384. Ibid

385. Jessica, Gloria Steinem on Feminism, Sarah Palin: "It's Such an Insult." Jezebel, hyyp://jezebel.com/5056307/glories-steinem-on-feminism-sarah-palin, Sept 29, 2008.

386. See, e.g., Steinem, Gloria, *Revolution from Within:A Book of Self-Esteem, Outrageous Acts and Everyday Rebellions, Moving Beyond Words, and Marilyn: Norma Jean.*

387. Marcello, Patricia. Gloria Steinem:A Biography.Westport, CT: Greenwood Press, 2004.

388. The Harvey Walker Agency biography of Gloria Steinem, http://www.harrywalker.com/speaker/Gloria-Steinem.cfm/

389. Steinem, Gloria, Wrong Woman, Wrong Message, Sept 6,2008,Women against Sarah Palin,http://womenagainstsarahpalin.blogspot.com/2008/09.

390. Ibid.

391. Ibid.

392. Yahoo News room, Transcript of Obama's acceptance speech. Nov. 5, 2008. http://news.yahoo.com/s/ynews/ynews_p1135.

393. Ibid

394. Ibid

395. See, Arnold, Matthew, Ibid.

396. Webster's New World college dictionary, Fourth Edition, Wiley Publishing, 2002.

397. U.S. Census Bureau, Facts for Features: Women's History Month-March 2008. www.Prnewswire.com/cgi-bin/stories.pl?acct=104&story

398. Ibid

399. Ibid

400. Ibid

401. Ibid

402. Ibid

403. Frith, Maxine,Life Expectancy rises to 81 for women but gap between rich and poor widens;   High Beam Research, Nov. 22,2006. www.highbeam.com/doc/1P2.

404. U.S. Census Bureau, Jan 26, 2006, Women-Owned Businesses Grew at Twice the National Average, Census Bureau Reports. Mike Bergman reports. www.census.gov/Press-Release/www/releases/archives/business.

405. U.S. Census Bureau, Facts for Features: Women's History Month-March 2008. www.Prnewswire.com/cgi-bin/stories.pl?acct=104&story for features apecial.

406. Ibid

407. Ibid

408. Altinkemer, Cheryl, Applying the Rule of Seven to Gift Planning, www.pgdc.com/pgdc/article/2001/09/applying rule seven gift planning. Planned Design Gift Center

409. Smith, Joyce, Marketing Expert Offers Tips on Selling to Women, Kansas Women's Business Center,Kansas City Star web site. See also, Winning the Toughest Customer: The Essential Guide to Selling to Women

410. U.S. Census Bureau, Facts for Features, Jan.2, 2008, Press Release, www.census.gov/Press-Release/www/releases/archives/facts

411. U.S. Census Bureau, Facts for Features: Women's History Month-March 2008. www. Prnewswire.com/cgi-bin/stories.pl?acct=104&story for features apecial

412. U.S. Census Bureau, Facts for Features, Jan.2, 2008, Press Release, www.census.gov/Press-Release/www/releases/archives/facts

413. Institute for Women's Policy Research, Id.

414. www.abc.net.au/news/stories/2008/10/24, Obama rushes to see grandma to avoid past 'mistake'.

415. U.S. Census Bureau, Jan. 5, 2009, Facts for Features http://www.census.gov/Press-Release/www/releases/archives/facts; US. Census Bureau, March 2006, Facts for Features, http://www.census.gov/press-release/www/releases/archives/facts; U.S. Census Bureau, http://www.census.gov/Press-Release/www?releases/archives; http://www.femisex.com/content/femistats-voter-turnout-2008;

416. Ibid.

417. Ibid.

418. Women's Health usa, 2008, http://mchb.hrsa.gov/whusa08/hstat/hi/pages/207le.html.; See also, Women's Life Expectancy Drops Across U.S. April 22, 2008, http://www.cbsnews.com/stories/2008/04/22/health/main

419. U.S. Census Bureau, Jan. 5, 2009, Facts for Features http://www.census.gov/Press-Release/www/releases/archives/facts; US. Census Bureau, March 2006, Facts for Features, http://www.census.gov/press-release/www/releases/archives/facts; U.S. Census Bureau, http://www.census.gov/Press-Release/www?releases/archives; http://www.femisex.com/content/femistats-voter-turnout-2008

420. Ibid.

421. Associated press photo, www.pe.com/.../03Obama%20Inauguration(8).html

422. Associated Press, Turkeys slaughtered as Palin addresses media, video shows bloody work while Alaska governor describes turkey pardon, Nov. 21, 2008, http://www.msnbc.msn.com/id/27841028/; see also, http://www.youtube.com/watch?v=Mu785cJgG-w.

423. The Centrist Voice, http://centristvoice.wordpress.com/2008/11/01/palin-prank-called-by-can adian talk-show ; see also, http://www.youtube.com/watch?v=T19DeRkVY8w

424. Ibid.

425. Ibid.

426. On Oct. 30, 2009, see http://aim.search.aol.com/search/search/search?query=palin + joke& page=28&nt=SG28&s_it=tb.

427. Licino, Hal, 75 Sarah Palin Joke One Liner "Quotes," http://hubpages.com/hub/75-Sarah-Palin-Joke-One Liner -Quotes.

428. http://www.huffingtonpost.com/2009/10/29/rachel-maddow-ex-plores-pa_n_338458.html

429. Ibid.

430. http://www.youtube.com/watch?v=86NVZZwt7dU

431. http://www.youtube.com/watch?v=cz4omw8FrTM

432. The Nobel Peace Prize 2009-Press Release, http://nobelprize.org/nobe._prizes/peace/laureates/2009/press.html.

433. Ibid.

434. Obama, Barack, "Still Fired Up," Id.

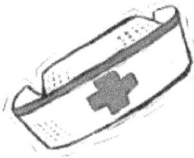

Registered
Nurse

Mother

Attorney

Author

Meet Malia Litman

Malia Litman is best known as the author of Rebuttal to the Rogue, which resulted from her passion for women's issues, and her commitment to educating women regarding candidates for political office.

Malia grew up in a very modest home in Tulsa Oklahoma, with her four siblings. Sharing the responsibility of college tuition, Malia worked various jobs as nurses aid, gift wrapper, and making cold calls for an insurance salesman.

Nursing was her first love, and she graduated with a Bachelor of Science Degree in Nursing. Realizing that nursing would not allow her the independence that she sought, Malia went on to Law School at O.U. While in Law School, Malia worked as a Registered Nurse in ICU, and the Burn ICU. In her third year of law school she taught Business Law to undergraduates in the Business School at O.U.

Probably due to dyslexia, Malia had difficulty getting admitted to Law School. After clearing the waiting list, Malia began her studies at O.U. Law School. She graduated in the top 10% of her class, was awarded an American Jurisprudence Award, she was a member of the O.U. Law Review, and the Moot Court Team. Malia was selected by the faculty as the "Outstanding Law Student" from her graduating class. Upon entering the practice of law, Malia specialized in litigation, becoming a Board Certified Trial Attorney. She achieved the position of Senior Partner with the prestigious Dallas law firm of Thompson & Knight. Malia was a frequent speaker at Continuing Legal Education Programs around the state of Texas, where fellow attorneys were her audience. She enjoyed the reputation of being a very successful trial attorney.

Twelve years after beginning her career, Malia made the difficult decision to "opt out" of her career to devote herself to raising her three children and ensuring the success of her marriage.

Fourteen years later, Malia has two kids in college, and a third in High School, none of whom have been incarcerated, rushed to the hospital for alcohol poisoning, or attended high school graduation with a baby in tow. Malia is still married to her first husband of 25 years. In 2008, Malia was happy with her family but not with the state of the country. For the first time in her life, Malia became involved in politics, working locally in Dallas, and for a short time in Ohio, to ensure the election of Barack Obama. Even though Malia never aspired to become an author, she felt passionately that women around the country should take note of the accomplishments of women in the election of 2008.

As a former trial attorney Malia was accustomed to making people accountable for the truth of what they said, and in the event Malia saw things differently than a witness, it was her job to present the opposing side, and let the jury/audience be the judge. Rebuttal to the Rogue is Malia's attempt to ensure that all the facts are presented regarding Sarah Palin, and give you the opportunity to be the judge.

www.ingramcontent.com/pod-product-compliance
Lightning Source LLC
Chambersburg PA
CBHW021341290326
41933CB00037B/321